STEPPING INTO THE SHADOWS

Why Women are Converting to Islam

Rosemary Sookhdeo

Stepping into the Shadows
Why Women are Converting to Islam

Published by Isaac Publishing. The Old Rectory, River Street, Pewsey, Wiltshire SN9 5DH United Kingdom

First Edition published in United Kingdom May 2005
Second Edition published March 2007

Scripture quotations are taken from the Holy Bible New International Version Copyright 1973, 1978, 1984 by International Bible Society. Inclusive language version 1995, 1996. Used by permission of Hodder and Stoughton Publishers. A member of the Hodder Headline Group. All rights reserved.

All quotations from the Qur'an unless otherwise stated are from The Meaning of the Glorious Qur'an translated by Mohammad Marmaduke Pickthall (Birmingham:UK Islamic Mission Dawah Centre 1997)

All quotations from the Hadith from Sahih Al Bukhari in the Alim (Silver Spring, Maryland USA: ISL Software Corp, 1986-2000)

ISBN   0-954835-7-3   978-0-9547835-7-0

Cover design by permission of Hänssler Publishing

Printed in the United Kingdom by Biddles Ltd, Kings Lynn.

ACKNOWLEDGEMENTS

I would like to thank the courageous women who were willing to have their stories told in this book. All names have been changed and parts of their stories have been omitted for their safety.

ABOUT THE AUTHOR

Rosemary Sookhdeo has been married to Patrick Sookhdeo for 36 years. Patrick was from a Muslim background and converted to Christianity several years before they married. For over 30 years Rosemary has been involved in the lives of women who have married Muslims and this book is a reflection of her experience.

Table of Contents

INTRODUCTION

R ecently my husband and I were taking a meeting in a small city in New Zealand on "How to Understand Islam". It was a relatively remote place, and certainly out of the way. After this meeting a woman came to see me looking very worried and distressed. Then it came out: her daughter had just got engaged to a Muslim man, a refugee from Afghanistan who had recently arrived in New Zealand. The question she wanted to ask me was: what could she do about it? She couldn't understand how this had happened. Her daughter had been brought up in the church, attending Sunday school and later youth activities. What had gone wrong? After leaving school her daughter had been working amongst refugees and that was how she came to be in close contact with Muslim men.

This was not an isolated incident. After almost every church meeting we take, at least one person comes up to speak to me about a member of their family or a friend who has married, or is about to marry, a Muslim and as a result is converting to Islam.

Where is this phenomenon of Christian women marrying Muslims and converting to Islam happening? It is happening across the church and society at large. The Christian parents I meet come from a range of denominations; some are members of the Brethren, some are Anglican, some are Baptist, some are from other evangelical traditions. Their sons and daughters have been brought up within the Christian faith, and many have accepted Christ into their lives. They have been church members, have attended youth groups and have been an integral part of a church. They have then gone to university and attended the Christian Union. Some of these young people are now far from the Lord, and before their conversion to Islam were very much a part of the secular, post-modern culture of the West. One thing they still have in common is parents who are regular members of evangelical churches, who have brought them up in a strong Christian tradition, who love them and pray constantly for them.

However it is not only young people who are marrying Muslims or converting to Islam. After a church meeting in which my husband was speaking on "How Christians should understand Islam", a woman in her late fifties came to speak to him. Much to his amazement, she told him that the main purpose of her coming to the meeting was to become a Muslim, and she thought he would be able to tell her what to do. She was from a middle class background, just an ordinary woman who had looked at society and felt that it was crumbling and its moral basis was deteriorating. She had looked at the Church and felt that it had nothing to offer, so she began to look to Islam which she thought could be an alternative, as it appeared attractive from the outside. She was searching, and was willing to try anything that could give her spiritual satisfaction. She is representative of a number of men and women who are converting to Islam by default. Disillusioned with Christianity and society, they think this alternative will have the answer.

Another category of Christian women who are converting to Islam includes those who are either divorced or have become widowed and are very lonely. These are often women in their fifties or older. They are from the middle classes, they are educated, they own their home and are financially well off and it is because of their financial status they can be targets for marriage by Muslims and then conversion to Islam

I was present with my husband at a Christian leadership conference when he took a seminar on "How to understand Islam after 9/11". The conference was being held by a well known evangelical fellowship group which represents hundreds of churches, both in the United Kingdom and overseas. Once a year they bring the leaders together from all parts of the world for training and fellowship. It was in the middle of this seminar that a young man stood up and said to the six hundred people present that he wanted to become a Muslim. There were gasps of horror around the room, as no one could believe what they were hearing. How could a Christian in church leadership be saying this? Was it a joke? No; it was a very serious situation. My husband very wisely said that he was sure someone could help him after the seminar.

We tend to think that certain categories of people are immune from any notion of conversion to Islam, and some of those categories include church workers, church leaders and missionaries. But this is not so. In the 1980s I knew a woman missionary in Pakistan who was sent home because she had formed a relationship with a Muslim man. Relatively recently an evangelical missionary society had one of its missionaries in Africa convert to Islam. In another missionary family whilst the wife and children had returned home for a short while for family reasons, she received a letter from her husband in which he told her not to bother coming back. He said he had fallen in love with a Muslim girl and was going to marry her and convert to Islam.

All the examples I have quoted are typical of something that is becoming more and more common. Recently we were at a church in the East End of London and a friend of ours whom we have known for forty years mentioned that their daughter had been going out with a Muslim. There are Members of Parliament whose children have married Muslims. Lord Birt, the former director of the BBC, has a son who has converted to Islam. We have all heard of Jemima Khan who converted to Islam as a result of marrying Imran Khan, the former Pakistani cricketer. Then there was Princess Diana, who formed relationships first with a Pakistani surgeon and then with Dodi Al Fayed.

In the small town where I live, which has a population of just 4,000, I know of four girls who have married Muslims. Two of them are daughters of a retired vicar who was a missionary in the Middle East, one is the daughter of our neighbour and now lives in Oman and the fourth was married in Turkey and is in hiding with her daughter.

It is very difficult to know how many western or Christian women are converting to Islam, but it is a substantial number. My husband was speaking at a major Christian conference recently of about 300 people from different parts of Britain. When he asked for a hand count of those who knew someone who had converted to Islam, fifty per cent of the audience put their hands up. He has asked the same question a number of times in large meetings which draw people from wide areas and the count has been on average at least thirty per cent of those present. Figures have been circulated that 30,000 western people over the last ten years have converted to Islam, the majority of these being women. So what is the attraction of Islam?

1

I WAS LIVING A DREAM

Mary's story

It all started with an innocent holiday in a North African country with my friend, where I had gone for a time of rest and recovery in the sunshine and warmth. When I first met Qasim I was not interested in him at all, in fact I thought he was interested in my girlfriend. He was handsome, quick witted, funny and intelligent, though uneducated, but appearing very western. He had done well at school but was unable to go to secondary school as his family couldn't afford it. We had a communication problem as he spoke no English, only conversational French, whereas I spoke broken French. As we attempted to communicate he was attentive and thoughtful, and there just seemed to be something about him that was different from anyone else I had met, and I felt he was for me. Qasim made me feel that I was special. He had a way of talking that was not slick, not even measured, but innocent; not worldly but had purity about it. This was an absolutely new experience for me. When I think of my first trips to North Africa it was almost as if he was always one step ahead of me and I was led to believe all the

...he talked about God as though he was almost a Christian.

time that nothing was too much trouble. He also talked about God and, as a Christian and not knowing anything about the Muslim faith, I found that acceptable. In fact he talked about God as though he was almost a Christian. He was very moral and was correct in all aspects of getting to know me and behaved impeccably.

Because of the difficulty we had with communication I tried to find a medium through which we could understand each other and I could begin to understand the mind of an Arab. I searched the bookshops and libraries to find works

There must have been some frailty within me or some need of love that he recognised he could lock into.

on romantic love, and I eventually found some books in French and tried to read them to him to explain how I felt. One of these books had a story about a woman who falls in love with a poor man from the "wrong side of the tracks" and has to get to grips with the issues involved. She echoed what I felt about my life and showed me what my life would be with this man. Qasim went along with it as though it would be part of his life as well. He wept with joy as he couldn't believe he had found a woman who thought like this about romantic love. For a western woman to come across this situation, to me, was unheard of and I suddenly wondered if we had all missed something, as western men didn't behave in this way. Why was everyone keeping this wonderful Muslim way of life a secret, when it was obviously so much more enjoyable? There must have been some frailty within me or some need of love that he recognised he could lock into.

Qasim had several visa applications refused to visit me in England and this was driving me insane. So I travelled back and forth many times, as I couldn't bear to think of this poor man struggling against the elements. I was desperate to get this relationship onto a regular footing, as I didn't want to be in a physical relationship without being married. A year after meeting we had a large wedding with many guests.

I Fell In Love With His Way Of Life

I went to where he lived and realised that it was not at all westernised. When I heard the muezzin calling to prayer, at that time it was exciting and romantic. I had always been interested in different cultures and realised that this new life was not one of material wealth, but wealth in

> **As I looked across this small village it was though I was looking across Bethlehem and for a Christian there was an amazing feeling of God.**

relation to the richness of family life and obedience to God. As I looked across this small village it was though I was looking across Bethlehem and for a Christian there was an amazing feeling of God. My cries to be nurtured and loved had been met as he reached the deepest part of my inner being.

In the village there were very old customs and ways, and I enjoyed the fact that I was living in a male orientated society, even though the men were quite controlling. The women had an unquenchable fighting spirit that I found admirable. But I was beginning to realise that the responsibility of my marriage to him included his family as well. I was told that if ever Qasim divorced he could never go back home, and that, for me was an assurance and a confidence that the marriage would last, as it was inconceivable that he could never visit his family again. The thought of divorce would bring shame upon his whole family. I wanted this marriage so desperately to work that there were many things that, in retrospect, I ignored.

Life In Britain

I expected our first year in Britain to be difficult, since Qasim was in a completely different culture. After a while he managed to get a job and began to hate the fact that he should support us as a family, as he thought that it was my responsibility. One of the most important things for him was to continue to send money back to his parents. We had managed to sort out the home in North Africa, and the place was transformed. I began to discover that it was my continuing duty to support his family back home but as I loved him so much I wanted to help all I could.

Qasim had no idea of what was expected of him in relationships in Britain. About two or three months after arriving in Britain he began to behave very strangely. He was wandering off on his own, and I thought that he was

I wanted this marriage so desperately to work that there were many things that, in retrospect, I ignored.

just exploring the town where we lived. He then began treating me as a sister or aunt and would shake my hand in the street and say he was going for a coffee. He would never kiss me. It was almost as though someone was watching him. To me this was odd behaviour as we had always done everything together.

Slowly I realised that he was beginning to organise his own life. He had a cobweb of contacts that I knew nothing about; a network of Arab men which he would visit – Libyans, Moroccans, Algerians and Saudis. I began to hear in his conversation anti-European and anti-western comments and he began to show how much he hated the fact that I was a Christian. After a few months in Britain I realised he was beginning to change and now, as head of the family, his word became law. He also assumed the headship of the extended family and in private family matters his views began to be obeyed. He seemed to find a new sense of power as he became more secure within himself, more autocratic and more selfish. He was not interested in me any more as a woman, let alone a wife.

As the months went on he began to be worried about his permanent visa to stay in Britain, as the embassy had already checked up on him to make sure he was still living with me. The tension of living in the West began to take its toll, along with the weather and the high cost of living. He began to goad me, and there were arguments when he said "How much longer have I got?" I used to laugh this off, but privately I began to worry that once his visa had arrived it would only be a short time before he left.

Qasim started to want to go out more and more on his

own and one night it all came to a head and he walked out. He came back later, even though I had hoped he wouldn't. His visa had not yet arrived.

When his permanent visa arrived his behaviour became even more distant and eventually, after another argument, he told me he was going to leave and that he would not be spending another night in the house. I was extremely distressed, wondering where he was going to go as I could not bear to think of him on his own wandering the streets. He also threatened me with physical violence which was another worrying aspect in the demise

When his permanent visa arrived his behaviour became even more distant and eventually, after another argument, he told me he was going to leave

of our relationship. I was at a loss to understand why our relationship had ended, and began to think back over the past years of my behaviour and wondered whether anything I had said or done had contributed to the break up of our marriage. Could it have been not enough money sent back home; was it conversations about intimacy; was it because he had not made many friends here or was it because he didn't like his job? Or did he feel threatened by me? In desperation I rang the Muslim women's helpline. They were at loss to know what to do.

I had thought that in some way our marriage could have been a bridge that would have helped both Christians and Muslims and I would have been happy for him to retain his Muslim faith. However I could never have relinquished my

Christian faith. But I really had thought that our relationship could have helped many people. Now I know this was only a romantic notion and I would have had to relinquish my faith, but I loved him so much I could sometimes almost have seen myself doing that.

What Went Wrong

I felt I did everything to accommodate Qasim and his family and feel now that the main purpose of our marriage had been for him to get a visa. It had all been a grand deception.

My life with him had become an emotional roller coaster and now I was completely drained. I still can't believe that I thought this man could meet all my emotional needs that I had as a woman. I always remember that as soon as we were married this romantic love on his part ceased.

He lied to me about his age and began to lie about the communications that I had sent to him. But how could I really have got to know him when he spoke so little English and how could I understand his family? These were all impossibilities. Qasim had a misconception of what the West had to offer as he expected life here to be similar to that at home but with every need being met because of the financial prosperity of the country. He had no concept of platonic friendships across the sexes and whenever I spoke to a man he thought I was having an affair.

Why was it that Qasim did not insist that I convert to Islam,

> **I always remember that as soon as we were married this romantic love on his part ceased.**

as this was quite usual if a western girl marries a Muslim? He didn't insist as it wasn't worth the effort, because for him the purpose for the marriage was to get into Britain. If a Muslim man is not serious about a long term marriage he makes no move to promote Islam. I was used simply for his own ends.

2

WHAT ATTRACTS WOMEN TO ISLAM

W hat is the attraction of Islam? Why is it that so many Christian girls, instead of being led up the aisle of a church to be married, are being led to the mosque? Why is it that western men and women are being converted to Islam by conviction?

Islam And Marriage

The main reason girls convert to Islam is that they fall in love with a Muslim man and end up marrying him. Some convert to Islam at the time of marriage, some convert at a later date, a few never convert at all but experience great difficulties if they want to follow Christ or bring their children up as Christians.

Falling In Love With A Muslim

The place where this is most likely to happen is in our universities and colleges, as it is here that relationships are forged across many cultural and racial barriers. Enjoying freedom from parental authority, often for the

The main reason girls convert to Islam is that they fall in love with a Muslim man and end up marrying him.

first time, a girl is able to pursue her own relationships away from the critical eyes of her family. It can be in naivety that she forms a friendship with a Muslim boy, in the same way she would with any of the other students. What she doesn't realise is that this form of friendship across the sexes doesn't exist within his culture.

By forming this friendship it is sending all the wrong signals to him as he thinks that she wants to proceed with a physical relationship, and is saying "come on". So as he becomes more and more friendly with her, he falls in love and develops the

Many women who marry Muslims marry within a short space of time, and engagements tend to be short.

relationship. Gradually she falls in love with him, oblivious to the implications of just being friendly. Sometimes the relationship can proceed so quickly that she has difficulty to extricate herself from it, and becomes trapped into marriage. Many women who marry Muslims marry within a short space of time, and engagements tend to be short. They usually meet and marry within the year.

The young Muslim man can appear very western, being away from his family and culture and seemingly behaving like every other student. He could be an overseas student from a Muslim country and, in a student environment, appear to behave in a western way. In this situation she can perceive little difference between his and her culture. However in Britain and other western countries there are also very many Muslim boys who have been born and brought up and educated in the west so can appear in all aspects to be the same as their western counterparts. Many don't appear to be bothered about their religion and having the first taste of freedom from parental restrictions can lead them into what is forbidden territory. At college or university they are now able to date western and other girls.

On her side the Muslim seems more exotic, more interesting, more caring and more romantic than other young men she has met. What she doesn't realise is that under the surface, the Muslim belongs to a totally different culture and a very different way of life, and it is not until after they are married that she begins to realise this. Before the marriage there were many things she thought wonderful, such as the close family ties, the welcome, and the hospitality. After the marriage she begins to realise that she hasn't just married an individual but has married a family and a community. What seemed wonderful before they were married slowly begins to take on another perspective. The girl I mentioned earlier who is engaged to the Afghan refugee is continually telling her mother how wonderful and close the family are, and how they have welcomed her.

A short while ago when we were taking a meeting in a church a woman came to me and said that her daughter had just married a Kurd. The mother had gone to Kurdistan for the wedding and said what a wonderful and close family they were. This is often the view of outsiders, but this perception totally changes when the outsider becomes an insider. Other girls engaged to Muslims have gone home and castigated their family for what they now perceive as poor family relations in their own home. They tell their parents that they should have had more loving homes.

Certainly there is nothing at all wrong with being interested in and appreciating other cultures, as Mary did on her visit to North Africa. It is good to admire the beauty and diversity of the world God has made. However, while we get alongside other people we must maintain our own identity as Christians, and our belief that everyone, from whatever culture, is equally in need of Christ.

"Diana Syndrome"

A number of the women who are attracted to Muslim men could be described as having "Diana syndrome". They are often from dysfunctional families, maybe their husband has left them or doesn't bother with them, and they are desperately unhappy. They are often emotionally unstable and are seeking happiness, or maybe they feel that they can't trust their husband and want some stability in their lives. Some have children. Women like this are very vulnerable and can easily be exploited, and they find in Islam a community and family that can care for them. These women are typified by Princess Diana; we think of her quest for happiness and how she searched for it – and maybe found it – with Muslim men.

Thankfully many vulnerable women find community, loving acceptance and a sense of belonging in a local church.

Sadly others do not find this to be their experience of the church.

Satu Typifies The "Diana Syndrome"

One person this "Diana syndrome" reminds me of is Satu. I have known Satu for many years, since she was a member of our church in East London. She came on Sundays to church and to the midweek coffee mornings with her little boy. She struggled as a Christian and never made church or the Lord a priority in her life. She was also very restless. As a church we tried to help both her and her husband and had very close contact with them as they seemed such a needy couple. Satu was born in Finland and came to Britain originally as an au-pair, looking for an escape and a chance of bettering herself. She had been a lively, unsettled and rebellious teenager desperately looking for stability and happiness. Her mother had died when she was young and she was brought up in what she considered to be an overly strict religious environment.

In Britain she met a handsome man who was a Greek Cypriot and fell desperately in love with him. They married and over the years had two children. We all knew that she had a difficult marriage, as her husband never really understood her and she never understood him or his culture. It was a marriage with severe cultural conflict and completely dysfunctional. Her husband was never home, and she believed he didn't really love her. She found housework and looking after children very boring. She was constantly out and soon began making friendships with other men.

One day she met a Muslim man who was very loving and caring to her, and she often stayed with him in his home.

In him she found the love, happiness and stability she so desperately sought. One day she decided to tell her husband that she was leaving him for this other man. This caused him to fly into a rage and attack her with a hammer, causing her serious injury. Aware of what he had done, her husband rang the police. Satu was airlifted to hospital, almost dead, and was unconscious for many weeks. Her husband was convicted and sent to prison.

When she recovered consciousness Satu found her new male Muslim friend at her bedside. He took her home, cared for her and asked her to marry him. This made her so happy that she shared her new joy with her friends and sought their approval.

After two years of marriage he left her because she was unable to produce any child for him.

Not many gave it. She married him and converted to Islam. After two years of marriage he left her because she was unable to produce any child for him. As soon as the divorce was through he married again and had a child. In Islam it is common for a man to divorce his wife if she cannot produce children, especially sons. In this situation a man may also take a second wife.

Satu is now in her fifties and lives alone in her East London flat with her two sons. When she goes out she puts on the hijab. She says she doesn't read the Qur'an and seems to know very little about Islam; in fact she really doesn't even know what it means to be a Muslim. But she has found in Islam a new community, new friends and a new way of life.

I think about this story with great sadness as I was involved with Satu for many years, and taught her Christian truths in the regular coffee mornings. I would never have believed that she would become a Muslim. What went wrong? Even though we taught her about Christianity, we never taught her about Islam and the differences between Islam and Christianity. In the end she had a choice and she chose a Muslim man and as a result Islam above her faith in Christ.

Targeted For A Visa

There are Muslim men who really want to live in the West, and they know that by marrying a western girl they can obtain their dream. I know of several women who married Muslim husbands who left them shortly after getting a permanent visa.

It is very common for Muslim men to target western girls for the sole purpose of a visa.

Muslim men who want to come to the West sometimes seek out western women on holiday in order to form relationships with them. We saw this in the story of Mary in chapter one. When women go on holiday, their guard may be down and they are looking for a good time, love and companionship. Many women meet their Muslim husbands while on holiday in places like Tunisia, Turkey, Morocco and Egypt. They fall in love and can't bear to be separated from them, so they marry in a very short period of time. It is very common for Muslim men to target western girls for the sole purpose of a visa.

Trapped Into A Marriage

Ali had come to Britain from Tunisia on a holiday visa and had been working in a restaurant, and it was there that Carol met him. She had gone to his restaurant for a meal with a group of her friends, and he had been very friendly and interested in her. She started to go out with him and a relationship began to develop.

Suddenly there was a crisis: his visa was expiring and he would have to leave the country, but he desperately wanted to stay. He told her how much he loved her and convinced her to marry him. They got married and then went back to Tunisia for a short visit, where they obtained a visa for him to return to Britain. She didn't tell her parents or friends that she was getting married. At this moment she is still working on the relationship, still unsure whether she wants to be married to him or not; and is in a dilemma. In fact she was trapped into marriage. This is not an uncommon story.

There are also girls who have become pregnant by a man who hasn't got permanent leave to remain in Britain. This can be a deliberate policy

There are also girls who have become pregnant by a man who hasn't got permanent leave to remain in Britain. This can be a deliberate policy, as a means to get residency. The man will go and live with the girl until he has his visa and then he will leave her.

Older Women And Muslim Men

It is not only younger women who are falling in love with

Muslim men, but women in their forties, fifties and older. These women are usually unmarried, divorced or widowed and are often financially well-off. What unites them all is that they are desperately lonely and looking for companionship and love. They go travelling to Africa or Middle Eastern countries and meet Muslim men, who they marry, some marrying men considerably younger. As western societies become more fragmented, with disastrous effects on families and communities, many women are looking for a sense of belonging. They are finding this in the Islamic context with the seeming welcome into families and communities.

The Internet

With the explosion in online dating, many women are seeking for husbands on the internet, and many are finding Muslim men and marrying them.

Recently a young woman came for an interview for a position in our ministry. Apart from work, she was doing a course of Bible study and was very keen to evangelise Muslims. She had found a chat room on the internet where she had started to share the Gospel with some Muslim men. Thrilled, she told how one Muslim man in Pakistan had accepted Christ and become a Christian and she was discipling him. I asked her if he was worshipping in a church and she said that he

One basic rule in evangelism to Muslims is that women can only evangelise women and men only men. To break this rule goes against every cultural norm of Muslim society.

wasn't. She mentioned how he had recently e-mailed her to say he was coming to Britain to visit his son at school and he wanted to meet her. I was concerned, because if he met her this relationship could easily get out of hand. It is difficult to determine over the internet if a person is a true believer, as some men are using this as a guise to marry western women and enter into western countries. One basic rule in evangelism to Muslims is that women can only evangelise women and men only men. To break this rule goes against every cultural norm of Muslim society.

3

I WAS DEFLECTED FROM MY MISSIONARY CALLING

I have known Helena from Finland for over twenty years. Helena found a home at St Andrew's and regularly attended the Tuesday coffee mornings and the Thursday women's meetings as well as the Sunday services for many years until she eventually moved house. She was a vital and valued church member with a gift for warmth and hospitality. Helena frequently welcomed me and many of our church members into her home it was there that I learned, to my distress, of the difficulties within her marriage and of the traumas she was suffering.

Helena's Story

I arrived in Tilbury in 1969 with my one suitcase and a clear guidance from the Lord to study nursing and then to work overseas as a missionary. I was twenty and had already been to Bible College and then had worked in a Mission Home as well as being involved in local outreach.

I thoroughly enjoyed my nursing training and then went on to study midwifery. I found the miracle of seeing a new life being brought into the world safely and the recovery of the mother very fulfilling. One day the death of a newborn child, too weak to face the struggle of life, greatly moved me.

I realised that preserving life and caring for those whose life was coming to an end was a precious calling.

During this time I lived in the East End of London. I was thrilled by the exciting experience of being in such a colourful place, full of activity as people from different ethnic groups thronged the markets and shops. My social circle began to widen as I met fellow students from many different countries and belonging to many different religions. When I first saw "Mustafa" in the local college my heart jumped. He looked so special. He was the handsomest man I had ever met and his manners and charming voice were immensely appealing.

He was the handsomest man I had ever met and his manners and charming voice were immensely appealing.

He didn't notice me but I watched him from a distance. He was very popular and, even though he had the reputation of being a womaniser, he dated many of my friends. I didn't tell anyone how he was constantly in my thoughts. Unexpectedly one day he rang the nurses' home and asked me out but I felt hurt that I was last on his list, so I refused and tried to forget him. It was to be three years before I saw him again.

Our Relationship Began After I Met Him In Church

I continued with my nursing training and started attending the Nurses' Christian Fellowship and the local church. The services were lively and vibrant with great singing and good teaching. Suddenly one Sunday Mustafa appeared at the church. I was pleased to see him - his was a familiar face in a sea of people and we started talking. We seemed to get on very well. I soon felt sure that now he was attending church and had accepted the Christian faith everything would be fine. We began to see each other frequently. After six weeks he proposed. I was blissfully in love. Nothing else seemed to matter. We were two young people in love and that was all that counted. However, one thing slightly marred my joy. Mustafa told me that if his family found out that I was white, and from a different country and race, they would stop us getting married. At the time I thought that this was a most unenlightened attitude. We obtained a special license to get married and had two strangers who were passers-by as our witnesses. I was determined that nothing or no-one would spoil our happiness.

In the early weeks of our marriage I soon realised that Mustafa was not very good at organising anything; he had made no plans for our life together. After getting married I was still living in the nurses' home and he was living with his

I soon felt sure that now he was attending church and had accepted the Christian faith everything would be fine.

brother. I had to make him write to tell his own mother in Pakistan that he was married. He claimed to have a degree from a university in Pakistan, but when he applied to study in Britain he failed to obtain a place on the course. After a while he began to work in an accountant's office as a clerk. He claimed to be able to buy a house for us to live in but this took many years to materialize. I desperately wanted security and a place of our own.

He Had Become A Christian But Family Pressure Proved To Be Too Great

A few months after the wedding I finally met his brother. The first time I met him he was friendly and very pleasant. However, Mustafa was bluntly reproved for marrying a white Christian woman and for attending church and was instructed that he must never go again. I was also forbidden to go to church. Mustafa obeyed and rejected Christ because of the family pressure and his behaviour changed from that day. Mustafa's brother also told me that we had to have an Islamic wedding. I knew very little about Islam, except that it contradicted the Bible, so I told him that I could not bow down to the Qur'an. That was the end of that discussion.

> **However, Mustafa was bluntly reproved for marrying a white Christian woman and for attending church and was instructed that he must never go again. I was also forbidden to go to church.**

As was the custom we went to live in the eldest brother's house where I was the only female. I wore Asian dress and settled into a life of housework, extended family togetherness and shopping in Asian food shops. Within one year of marriage I had our first child, a beautiful healthy baby daughter. To my consternation, my husband hung his head because, like all Muslim men, he wanted a boy. I had to tell him in no uncertain terms that he should be happy at the birth of our daughter. The two worlds had begun to collide. In a short time I had another child - a boy. This time Mustafa was happy and very proud. I felt that God had generously blessed us with the two beautiful children – a boy and a girl.

The Difficult Years Of Marriage

During the first two years of marriage I became aware that the man I had married was very short-tempered. He became increasingly irritable and dominating. He frequently boasted of his well-to-do family in Pakistan. He had a chip on his shoulder,

By now the charming, lovely man I had married had turned into a short-tempered tyrant.

constantly accusing the English of robbing his country and doing it harm. I tried to tell him that I came from a peaceful nation and should not be the object of his hate. I found his racist comments (as they appeared to me) to be very distasteful. I asked him to go and see the doctor as I felt he was clearly showing signs of stress. However, my advice merely made him more irate.

More of his family moved into our small three-bedroom house. It was cramped and we had very little privacy. Mustafa would occasionally come home smelling of alcohol and would snap at me. His brother would take my side and tell him off. By now the charming, lovely man I had married had turned into a short-tempered tyrant. The situation in the house became intolerable. Our own house was still a dream, so we applied for council housing.

A Breathing Space In The Marriage

At this time my father became very ill in Finland. I went

with the children to visit him so he could see more of his grand children as we knew he didn't have very long to live. The temporary parting with Mustafa was amicable. Whilst staying with my parents I went out to work to support us as no maintenance came from Mustafa. I thought that this space would allow him time to calm his state of mind. Little did I know what was in store for us!

A year later he came to Finland and we all returned to Britain together. On our return, terrible news awaited us. Mustafa was met by the local police. He had been traced through Interpol as a contact of someone with a communicable disease. After a few days I learnt that he had met a Finnish girl at a party; who was now in hospital suffering from the disease. He spun me an unbelievable story in order to try and excuse himself and this lead to a massive argument. This distressing experience was a traumatic shock and nearly ended our marriage. Any trust I had in him was gone forever. Now I pitied and despised him.

A Deteriorating Marriage

Life became more difficult as Mustafa didn't like spending time at home; the domestic scene irritated him. He was exasperated by the children playing and their voices annoyed him. He didn't like my cooking. He was unhelpful, refusing, for example, to go and buy the meat from the Halal butcher. This was very embarrassing for me as only men went into this shop. Mustafa told me to tell the butcher that he didn't like queuing in the shop because of the smell of raw meat. The butcher gave me questioning looks – I could see he thought it strange that I and not my husband came to the shop.

When Mustafa's mother, Amatzi, arrived from Pakistan, I felt an instant liking for her. She was a down–to-earth, strong woman and taught me how to cook curries and make chapati's. One Sunday afternoon, when the whole extended family was present for Sunday lunch, she told them that I was very like her when she was young, as she was hard-working and had tried to look after her family and husband well. She then added that I was better than her other daughters-in-law. This brought conflict and division between me and the rest of his family that would never be forgotten.

This brought conflict and division between me and the rest of his family that would never be forgotten.

We finally moved to East London into what must have been the second cheapest house in the borough, which we gradually improved. Mustafa was still suffering from stress and refused to go for help; instead, he started staying away for whole weekends, hanging around at Marble Arch in questionable company.

A Road Accident And The Consequences

Two days before my final exams for nursing I was involved in a serious road traffic accident whilst accompanying a patient to another hospital. I suffered a serious and lasting neck injury that ended my nursing career. The compensation money helped to pay the bills. The child I was carrying at the time of the accident was lost one month later, but within a year I was to have another baby boy.

After my accident I carried on as best I could to keep

the house and cook. Mustafa refused to help in any way even though I was in need of complete rest as my spine was affected by the accident. The injury caused terrible headaches and vertigo, and every step I took jarred my body from my heels to my head. As I could no longer work, money became a problem as there was now less coming in and the budget was tight. In spite of this, Mustafa continued to send money to Pakistan. Any objections I voiced just led to arguments, at which he would walk out of the house, and not return for a long time. He would shout at me and make me feel worthless and I felt I had been relegated to the role of housekeeper.

By the time the fourth child was on the way Mustafa was becoming so verbally and physical abusive that I had to sleep in a separate room. He was shouting constantly at the children, especially at our eldest son who one day developed severe stomach pains with suspected appendicitis. I wanted him to go to the doctor but Mustafa refused to take him by car, so I had to pick him up, despite being heavily pregnant and suffering from my severe neck injury, and carry him there myself. As I went out through the door, Mustafa struck me a violent blow on the back of my head. A few days later he tried to kick me in the stomach. Our eldest son bravely stood up against him and shouted at him not to hit me, then, in fear, ran upstairs to hide from his father who was chasing him. The Lord gave me the strength to stand up to Mustafa and stop him from beating him

Mustafa Tries To Destroy My Faith
By now I was going to church on an occasional Sunday morning, feeling very low and tearful, too frightened to live

in the same house as Mustafa and desperately worried about the future. I needed the comfort of hearing Bible teaching and singing the familiar hymns. Mustafa was furious about my going to church and began to have terrible temper tantrums. My attendance at church was so enraging to him that he did everything he could to destroy my faith. He tore up my Bible. He believed my place was at home to be at his beck and call every Sunday morning and to get his food, but then he would go off for the rest of the day. Whatever I wanted to do was irrelevant and he began to be extremely jealous when I went out. He even began to accuse me of having affairs, which was completely untrue. I began to see that his problem was much more than stress at work or unwillingness to be a responsible father and husband; I realised that he no longer had any love for me.

> **Mustafa was furious about my going to church and began to have terrible temper tantrums. My attendance at church was so enraging to him that he did everything he could to destroy my faith. He tore up my Bible.**

The Inevitable Divorce

I had to obtain two court orders to get him out of the marital home. The divorce took two years to come through, and Mustafa tried every possible way to discredit me in the court and to get custody of the children. All his attempts failed. One day a distant female relative of his called on me and tried to get the family to go to her house, which set off warning bells as to whether this were an attempt to abduct the children.

About this time I met my sister-in-law in the street and was told that I should just accept my husband hitting me.

Mustafa twice asked me to take him back, crying on the phone and asking for forgiveness but saying that he had done nothing wrong. I felt pity for him so invited him around for a visit. The children were alarmed to see him and his behaviour was so upsetting and destructive that they refused to see him, let alone live with him, again.

Both of Mustafa's parents and his eldest brother have since died. He married again and his second wife, who was from Pakistan, aborted their child and cost him a great deal in legal expenses in their divorce. His third wife is a village

...I met my sister-in-law in the street and was told that I should just accept my husband hitting me.

girl from Pakistan, a relative, and yet he still continues to have affairs with other women. Mustafa now suffers from anxiety attacks and is a broken old man.

In Conclusion

My life has not been smooth. People have let me down, and I have been in and out of hospital. Yet, looking back now, I can see that my experiences have been valuable and have brought me many spiritual benefits. I feel that meeting Mustafa and getting married was right and God blessed us with beautiful and intelligent children. On several occasions I learnt of the authority I had walking as a child of God as many times there was a very clear confrontation with the forces of evil. My faith grew stronger and clearer and I had no doubts.

My commitment to Christ continued to grow through the bleak days when I began to learn that Mustafa was a bitter person, a liar and a cheat. He boasted of his wealth; the children and I saw nothing of it. I confronted him with the fact that his brothers, on a lower salary than us, could afford their own homes and cars and their wives didn't have to work. I had to go to work for us to get anything at all. He always got angry and avoided a clear answer. Mustafa

He was always a people-pleaser to get benefit for himself.

had no depth. When he was confronted by his brother about going to church he did not stand firm but went along with his brother's demands. The little faith he had acquired was denied by his failure to witness and to speak up for what he believed. He would rather keep his inheritance.

In every commitment he was superficial. He was always a people-pleaser to get benefit for himself. Over the years of our marriage his behaviour grew worse as did his lies, anger and violence. He often seemed like a man who was haunted. I saw the hatred in his eyes for me; there was no care or compassion. I was determined that I was not going to be destroyed by someone who seemed to be suffering from bouts of temporary insanity, nor could I allow my children to be subjected to it.

The stigma of divorce was not easy to endure. I cried so much in the early years that in the end I felt numb. But God in his grace spoke to me through words of comfort from the pages of my Bible: "Do not cry, you who are desolate. I will make you a happy mother in the house with your children". And it came to be. I came to understand my difficult experiences as clashes and wounds received in the wars. God's word says, "He trains ones hands for the battle". I came to realise how many others have faced much worse situations and have not bowed to false gods or denied Jesus. Mustafa rejected Christ by surrendering to the wishes of his family and his peace left him.

Through my suffering the Lord has given me the strength to stand up for what is right with honesty and integrity. I know the teachings of the Bible are supreme. Jesus, even though human, was sinless with no stain on his character; he was the Son of God.

Mustafa rejected Christ by surrendering to the wishes of his family and his peace left him.

Jesus' teachings to me have been like water in the desert, comfort to the soul and have given me courage in my weakness, peace and contentment in the midst of all my troubles.

My life is very full now. The children have grown up and I have many friends and now help in my church. The painful years during my marriage taught me how precious faith in Jesus is, even as Mustafa tried to destroy it by whatever means he could. It was during those dark years that the Lord sent good friends to encourage, help and support me. I received numerous answers to prayer and knew the power and the presence of the Holy Spirit. I might be poor now but I am free.

Fooled Into Believing He Was A Christian

In Helena's story Mustafa seemed to be genuinely seeking

God and he did make a commitment to the Christian faith. However the family pressure was very great and ultimately family came first. His becoming a Christian brought shame on the family. Many women have believed that the men they were marrying had accepted Christ into their lives, but as soon as they were married the commitment evaporated away. The "commitment" was actually a tool that would convince the Christian woman that it was right to marry them. The woman could see the conversion as a sign from God. Christian women do need to be wise and careful in relating to men who have very recently converted from Islam, being aware that the cultural norms of Muslim culture, as mentioned above, have little place for platonic friendship between men and women.

I am not saying "Do not marry Muslim converts to Christianity". If a convert is established and going on in the faith before the woman met him that would be a totally different situation.

A story comes out of Germany of a girl who met a Muslim boy from Pakistan and prayed that he would become a Christian and then she would marry him. He didn't become a Christian, but she still married him and still continues to pray that he will find Christ. But what is worrying is that she seeks his conversion as a confirmation from the Lord that she has made the right decision in marrying him.

Some women do marry a Muslim man because they believe that if they pray, the Lord will save them and they will leave Islam. Whereas this in theory is possible, as nothing is too hard for the Lord, in practice it is a very rare occurrence.

Christians will be aware of the principle that a Christian should marry someone who shares their faith – and not someone who doesn't - but can be swayed by the feelings of falling in love. So they put a spiritual gloss on what they desire by talking of marriage to a Muslim as a way to

> **They do not realise that when they marry they will have to give up their individual freedoms, as they will be marrying into a family and a community**

convert him, or of building a bridge of understanding between two faiths. Sometimes, by the grace of God, it happens, but that doesn't mean the marriage was the right thing to do. Much more often it leads to gradually stepping out of God's light.

Emphasis On Community

Another attraction of Islam is the emphasis on community and family. The close-knit ties and bonds offer an attractive alternative to the individualism of western societies. However the downside of this is that close communities can be oppressive and deny individual freedom. Western women desiring community do not always see these negative aspects of it. They do not realise that when they marry they will have to give up their individual freedoms, as they will be marrying into a family and a community which dictate behaviour and function.

Central to this concept of community is the mosque. For Muslims it is the central pivot of the community and is a political, spiritual and social entity giving identity and purpose. Many activities go on inside and around the mosque such as feeding the poor, education, and counselling, and it is open every day. There are meetings for women with special speakers and informal meetings in homes with food and warm hospitality.

Some Convert Because They Think Islam And Christianity Are Very Similar

Some women convert to Islam because they are not aware of the differences between Islam and Christianity. They think both religions are very similar, so it doesn't matter which one you follow. Muslims speak about God and Jesus, how Jesus had a virgin birth, was sinless, performed miracles, and ascended into heaven and they also mention many of the prophets of the Old Testament, the end times and subjects such as praying and fasting and reciting the creed. People are confused, because to hear these subjects mentioned it could be a Christian speaking. Many women convert to Islam on marriage thinking there is very little difference between the religions.

There is no assurance of salvation no matter how hard a person strives.

People often ask whether Allah and God are the same. Some people believe that they are the same and therefore both ways lead to the same goal. But the important question is not whether Muslims and Christians believe in the same God, but what they believe about God's character. Christians understand the nature of God by looking at Christ who revealed the extent of God's love for humanity. They believe God's primary attribute is love and call him Father. Islam stresses God's greatness, transcendence, otherness and might. God is so "other" that he cannot be adequately described in human language neither can he enter into humanity, so he is unable to suffer. He is distant and "wills what he wills", which could be either good or evil. There is no assurance of salvation no matter how hard a person strives.

4

CONVERSION BY CONVICTION

Simplicity Of Understanding

One attraction of Islam is that the practices and beliefs of the religion are set out simply and are very easy to understand. Islam is not a complex religion. It is in fact a set of rules. It tells you how to pray, when to pray, how to fast, when to fast, what to believe, how much money to give and so on. It is all laid out clearly. Some people are attracted by this simplicity of belief, with everything set out and organised for them. Its creed is very simple – "There is no god but God and Muhammad is his messenger". Muslims must recite this creed at least once a day.

Some women convert to Islam because they believe that it is genuinely the right path to finding God. These are women who are aware of a spiritual vacuum within their lives, or they can be people who are very lonely and looking for friendship. They are usually introduced to the religion by a Muslim friend or acquaintance and can be recruited at universities or colleges by groups of friendly and enthusiastic

One attraction of Islam is that the practices and beliefs of the religion are set out simply and are very easy to understand.

Muslims who take them to their meetings.

The majority of young people converting to Islam are from middle-class backgrounds, many from Christian homes, and the young men that are converting are often from the upper classes, from top public schools and universities. In this group there has always been a tendency to do something different and to break the mould; for example, it was from this class that the spies of the last century came.

A Meeting Arranged By God

Some thirty-six years ago, when I was a theology student in London, some of us decided we would like to go on holiday over the summer break. This was a spur of the moment decision and as we wanted to travel the next day we realised our choice would be limited. The only cheap rail tickets we could get were to

The majority of young people converting to Islam are from middle-class backgrounds, many from Christian homes

Naples. It is amazing, years later, to see how that decision was truly of the Lord and what happened subsequently.

We boarded the train to Naples and took our seats, which were four seats facing each other, and waited to see who the fourth person would be. It was a long arduous journey of about twenty-nine hours, trying to sleep sitting upright with noise unabated from the rest of the carriage. Meals were difficult, and the whole journey turned into an endurance test.

Sitting in the fourth seat was a young man called John who lived in England, and by the time we reached Naples we had become friends. He was not a Christian, but was from a Christian background and at the end of the journey we exchanged addresses. Over the years, but not frequently, John kept in touch with us and he came to visit us on several occasions. One day he rang out of the blue with the wonderful news that he had become a Christian and we rejoiced that he had found the Lord. At a later date he came to see us to share that his sister Miriam had become a Muslim and could we pray for her. Years later after she had found the Lord, John took me to visit her and I had burning questions that I wanted to ask her.

I Found Allah Was Not A God Of Love
Miriam's Story

When my mother died in 1977 I felt abandoned by God and vulnerable. I hated God. I blamed Him for causing me to lose not only my very best friend but also my greatest support in life. I was living at home at the time and was grief-stricken. I also had to come to terms with the shock of my father marrying again in the space of six short weeks. My parents had known Rose many years ago, before I was born. My brothers and I never knew her. She was from Australia and as far as I was concerned was a stranger from another country and it seemed as if she was taking the place of my mother and running the household. That year I left home to go to college, my life in tatters. For a long time I was searching for some kind of stability in my relationships but without success. I met Neil and in 1984 we became husband and wife.

The Beginning Of An Interest In Islam

It was five years later when Neil and I were on holiday in Turkey that I experienced the first inklings of an interest in Islam. I was mesmerized by the beauty of the mosques and spellbound as I heard the call to prayer during the set times of the day.

I was mesmerized by the beauty of the mosques and spellbound as I heard the call to prayer during the set times of the day.

There was one particular mosque I was drawn to. It was very old and its architecture seemed unusual for this part of the world. As we stood in the central courtyard surrounded by the ruins, I was very surprised that amongst all this chaos a small section of the mosque had been restored and was in use. I felt an amazing sense of calm and contrasted my life which was spiralling out of control with the peace I found inside this building. At this point in time I was not a Christian and neither Neil nor I had any interest in following a religion.

A month later, as a surprise, Neil went out and bought me an English translation of the Qur'an. I shall never know why he did this. It was so special to receive this Qur'an -perhaps because it reminded me of our holiday in Turkey. I started to read it. I also began to love everything about the cultural side of Islam, attracted by the sheer beauty of the architecture, the designs and patterns. My interest in Islam had begun.

Life In Turkey

A year later, Neil and I split up. I was determined to go back to Turkey so the following year I went on my own and stayed in a beautiful place called Kusadasi. Here the local people looked after me and protected me. For example, when I went into town they wouldn't let me go alone and insisted that I take a chaperone. It was lovely. I contrasted my experience back home in England to my experience here. I thought that if this was what Islam was all about – caring for you and protecting you - then I was indeed attracted to it. My second year in Turkey was wonderful. I will always remember it. What struck me was the welcome the Turkish people gave me and the relaxed freedom I found in the dress and life of the women.

Reluctantly I went back to England and there I met Ahmed from Algeria, and my interest in Islam grew and grew. When Ahmed visited his family in Algeria I took the decision to become a Muslim. I liked the security of it. I now felt more secure

> **I couldn't reconcile my present life with the life of my family so I began to live a double life.**

than at any time since my mother's death. Even during those terrible days after her death, much as I had hated God I had always acknowledged that he existed. But how could I accept him as a loving God after everything he had supposedly done to me? All I could see was that he had taken the one person who was the anchor in my life, my mother.

A Jekyll And Hyde Existence

After taking the decision to become a Muslim, a new problem arose. I had to try to live two separate lives - one for my family and one for my Muslim friends. It was like a Jekyll and Hyde existence. As long as I didn't think of my family I survived well, but when I met or thought of them I acknowledged there was a clash of cultures. I couldn't reconcile my present life with the life of my family so I began to live a double life.

Ahmed and I moved to London to "seek our fortune" but it was not long before our relationship was over when the promised job opportunities didn't materialise. I was left on my own once again.

Involvement With The Mosque

I started to learn Arabic and went to classes at the mosque, where I met a girl who

...I was not a complete Muslim until I adopted the hijab or stepped out into the world to show that I was a Muslim.

was to become a close friend. Deena welcomed me into her home and it was there I was to meet a friend of her husband called Stephen. Stephen was a convert from a Jamaican background who was born and brought up in London. It was suggested that he would make a good husband for me.

I attended the meetings where the Muslim sisters would discuss a whole range of topics. These discussions impressed upon me that I was not a complete Muslim until I adopted the hijab or stepped out into the world to show that I was a Muslim. In order to be identified as a Muslim, therefore, I started to wear the hijab but I felt I had to hide this from my family as they would not have understood.

As time went on and I learned more and more about Islam I began to realise how far short of the mark I was and that I could never reach it whatever I did. It was not as though cracks were appearing in my faith in Islam I loved the formal praying five times a day. It was a structure I could follow and

I needed this. But I started to feel that I could never climb the mountain before me or ever be good enough to get to paradise. I read in the Qur'an that in hellfire there are mostly women, and this was depressing me. The emptiness within me was growing and I was searching for answers and wondering if this religion is so good why do I think this way?

My Brother's Visit

In August 1997 when my brother John came to visit I was still convinced of the truth of Islam. He was shocked and saddened to see how much I had changed since we last met and he tried hard to share the Gospel message with us both but we were blinded by our devotion to Islam.

I had been a Muslim for nearly three years, and on the surface I was content and happily married to a kind, considerate and caring husband. I had married Stephen the Jamaican convert and we were expecting our first child. Life seemed complete, but deep inside I was troubled. There were times when I wondered whether God really loved me. In Islam Allah has ninety-nine names describing his qualities and nature but not one of these describes him as a God who loves. I had always known that, but now I really wanted him to love me

Life seemed complete, but deep inside I was troubled. There were times when I wondered whether God really loved me. In Islam Allah has ninety-nine names describing his qualities and nature but not one of these describes him as a God who loves.

and I began to feel that all my efforts were inadequate. What could I do to stay on the straight path and earn that precious place in heaven? Yet I was trying so hard to please him – I prayed five times a day, and I wore the headscarf and outer covering of a typical Muslim woman and I tried desperately to learn Arabic, which I found particularly hard.

Nagging Questions And Doubts

My daughter Salima was born the following January. As I began to adjust to my new role of first-time Mum those old nagging questions and doubts slowly and surely came flooding back to the surface. I started to switch on the television on a Sunday evening to watch Songs of Praise, something I had not done for a long time. I even started to sing along with the old familiar hymns that reminded me of my childhood. How strange that a Muslim woman should consider singing "Praise My Soul the King of Heaven" and "The King of Love My Shepherd Is"! There it was again - the word "love". In my heart I felt sure that God must be a God of love, as all people need to feel that they are loved and I am no exception. Little by little I began to read less of the Qur'an. One day I picked up the old Bible I had kept for some reason and started to read it. I was so captivated by it that I couldn't put it down, as for the first time in my life it seemed to be alive and speaking to me.

I read from the book of the prophet Isaiah who wrote about Jesus the Messiah six hundred years before his birth. As a Muslim I had accepted Jesus as a prophet who had been given the power to heal by Allah, but now I realised He was far more than this. In Isaiah 9:6 I read about a child who would be born and who would be called "Wonderful Counsellor, Mighty God, Everlasting Father, Prince of Peace". I wrestled with this thought for some time. Could this really be about Jesus? I also read Isaiah 53:3 ... "He was despised and rejected by men ... He was pierced for our transgressions, he was crushed for our iniquities; the punishment that

> **As a Muslim I had accepted Jesus as a prophet who had been given the power to heal by Allah, but now I realised He was far more than this.**

brought us peace was upon him". Here was an Old Testament prophet reminding me of the crucifixion story that I had heard many times as a child.

I began to read about the history of the Bible, how it is a collection of books put together over a period of about 1500 years by some 40 authors who were inspired by God. Second Timothy 3:16 so beautifully describes it "All Scripture is God-breathed". How different it is from the Qur'an, which claims to be the direct words of God given to Muhammad by the angel Gabriel.

I also read about the Dead Sea Scrolls where in 1947 complete texts of some of the Old Testament books, including that of Isaiah, and fragments of the rest were discovered by Bedouin shepherds. I learnt that our present day translations were indeed consistent with these ancient texts which have been scientifically dated to be around 200BC to 100AD. I had read many times in Islamic literature how the Bible had been corrupted and changed since the time of Jesus, but with evidence like this I seriously began to doubt that this was true.

Jesus The Messiah The Son Of God

I could no longer believe that Jesus was only a Prophet, he was certainly much more than that. I read again the Gospels about his life, his preaching, his crucifixion and resurrection. Jesus spoke of himself as the Way, the Truth and the Life. I read John 3 16-17: "For God so loved the world that he gave his one and only Son, that whoever believes in him shall not perish but have eternal life. For God did not send his Son into the world to condemn the world, but to save the world through him". At last I realised that God did indeed love me - and how he loved me! All I knew was that no matter what I believed as a Muslim, I now believed that Jesus was more than just another prophet; he was indeed God's son and no matter what the cost I had to accept him into my life and let him take control. I read in Romans 3:20 and 22, "no-one will be declared righteous in God's sight by observing the law ...

> **I read John 3 16-17: "For God so loved the world that he gave his one and only Son, that whoever believes in him shall not perish but have eternal life.**

This righteousness from God comes through faith in Jesus Christ to all who believe".

Around this time (in fact it was the 8th of July 1998), I went to stay with my brother John and sister-in-law, Susan. That first evening, I remember it well, I felt so different. My brother and I went for a walk with my daughter and for the first time I felt I didn't have to wear my scarf. I felt liberated. My brother noticed straight away that I had changed. We sat down for a while and I simply blurted out that I had to have

Jesus in my life. It was such a relief to have told someone at last. My brother was both shocked and delighted. He knew that I would need a great deal of support so he put me in touch with a Christian fellowship and, in particular, with Katrina and Tim. I returned home, but managed to keep my new faith in Jesus secret only for a few short weeks.

I Could Keep My Secret No Longer

The time came when I couldn't keep my secret any longer even though I knew that it would probably cause a whole heap of problems for me. When I told my husband, he was very, very upset and I felt quite frightened. I spent the next week at John and Susan's house to let the situation cool down a little. This gave us some "breathing space". I met some lovely Christian people during my stay there. My husband asked me to return, which I did and I thought at first everything was going to sort itself out, but it was not to be and my husband left the next day. My husband had been advised that as I had become a Christian I was to be regarded as an apostate and as such our marriage was null and void, so he should leave the house immediately.

My husband had been advised that as I had become a Christian I was to be regarded as an apostate and as such our marriage was null and void, so he should leave the house immediately.

At first I found everything very hard. When I was living back in London my husband would visit us on occasions, even though he was not supposed to do so. He tried to persuade me to change my mind and revert back to being a Muslim. Although I am now alone and there are times when I feel very lonely, I have a wonderful relationship with my heavenly Father who loves and cherishes me so much that he allowed his only Son to suffer the punishment for my sins. And it's a relationship that is growing and developing. The Lord has been so good to me over the past few years, and I have made so many good friends through my fellowship and elsewhere. I have met other converts from Islam and I am encouraged to hear of other Muslims who are also coming to know how much the Lord loves them.

It is amazing really when I think how the Lord has been waiting all these years for me to accept him as he truly is. I was brought up in a church-going family and had the opportunity to learn of God's love from an early age, but it was not until I had been a Muslim for several years that I started to seek God and come to know for myself of his love for me. I do thank the Lord for patiently waiting for me.

Lessons Learnt

1. Despite regretting my involvement in Islam, I do believe that God allowed me to go through that time in order that I might come to know and trust Him by accepting Jesus as my Saviour and Lord.

2. Through the experience of having been a Muslim I now realise what freedom is really like.

3. I now have a heart for Muslim people that they might come to know Jesus as Lord and Saviour.

4. I hate the religion of Islam because I believe that it is a dark deception. We are told that Islam means "submission" and

"peace" but as I got deeper into Islam I found that there was no peace.

5. I loved the idea of the extended family which used to be the case in our society. I saw families all living together, grandparents, aunties and uncles, all contributing to family life. This appealed to me especially after losing my mother ….and is one of the strengths of Muslim society.

6. When I was having Saleema in hospital some Muslim "sisters" came to see me. I was so touched that they had come. But **they explained that they had come to visit me not because they liked me as a person, but to earn blessings from Allah.** Their visit was nothing to do with relationships or loving one another. I felt betrayed. This episode stuck in my mind and was instrumental in my questioning Islam.

7. I was told that my mother was in hellfire. This really hurt and upset me. It was also mentioned to me that when a Muslim man marries a Christian woman, if she dies a Christian, she goes straight to hell.

Advice For Anyone Marrying A Muslim Or Converting To Islam

I would advise anyone contemplating becoming a Muslim that they should find out as much as they can about Islam, not what they would like to believe, but the facts. This can be very difficult if you are in a relationship with a Muslim man and you don't want to hurt

I would advise anyone contemplating becoming a Muslim that they should find out as much as they can about Islam, not what they would like to believe, but the facts.

him. However, there are consequences for your future if you don't do this vital research. If you are determined to marry a Muslim man my advice is not to convert. Remember that in Islam a Muslim man is able to marry a Christian woman but not vice versa. The pressure is then on the woman. DON'T CONVERT JUST TO MARRY SOMEONE.

My Sister Miriam By Her Brother John

When I became a Christian in June 1994 I was anxious to tell everyone about my new-found faith and my sister Miriam was no exception. The many chats I had with her were by and large monologues as I tried to convince her to follow my path. My sister Miriam lived together with Ahmed from Algeria. I visited them on one occasion, and remember a particularly revealing conversation – revealing because of my ignorance of Islam at that time. I asked Ahmed what he would do if someone tried to harm Miriam. He replied that he would kill that person as Miriam was his property. I was shocked because they were not even married. Ahmed went home to visit his family in Algeria and it was during his absence that my sister rang me up to tell me that she had made the decision to become a Muslim.

The relationship with Ahmed didn't last and Miriam found herself living alone in London. It was at this time that she became involved with the local mosque and its various activities, making new friends. One day she took the decision that she would live as a Muslim woman with all that it would entail in terms of discrimination. However, whenever she went home to stay with the family she tried to hide this other life from our father, for example by not wearing the hijab. I was the only person in the family who knew and in whom she confided, as she was fearful of repercussions. At this time I went along with the situation even though I felt unhappy to keep it a secret. At the mosque she attended she was introduced to the man who had been chosen to marry her. Miriam was married under Islamic or Shariah Law with no civil ceremony alongside, as she was told it was considered unnecessary. Stephen, like herself, was a Muslim convert and was from a Jamaican background, his father being a Pentecostal pastor belonging to the Jesus-only sect.

I met Stephen for the first time at Miriam's home in London when I went to pay them a visit. Miriam met me at the station wearing the hijab, which shocked me. It was so out of keeping that it felt as though she was not my sister. Before I travelled to London I had found the church nearest to my sister's home and asked them to pray for us during that day. (This was the fellowship into which she "stumbled" after she became a Christian in July 1998. We praise the Lord that His ways are perfect, as this was the church that had been praying for her).

At the mosque she attended she was introduced to the man who had been chosen to marry her.

When I arrived at the house I met Stephen who embraced me as his brother. During my stay he told me something of his background, particularly of his relationship with his father. He mentioned how each Sunday morning the father gave the instruction that his three sons were to walk to church whilst he took the car, and if they were late he would beat them. This beating occurred many times. In fact the father had instilled fear in the rest of the family, as his motto was "not to spare the rod and spoil the child". With this background in mind it may not be surprising that the three brothers sought an escape from the iron grip of the father. Stephen found the escape in Islam.

When I visited Stephen and Miriam in August 1997 they were convinced Muslims, as far as I could tell. I tried to witness to them but Stephen knew enough about the Bible to counteract anything I said. At this time I was still trying to win

"I see a woman in Arab dress and the Lord is saying that he will take away the veil from her face so that she can see".

by force of argument and would have to learn to "speak about the truth in love". I left very disappointed, but in the train on the way home I met a group who were going to a Christian convention and we all prayed for Stephen and Miriam.

Shortly after the birth of their daughter Salima in January 1998 Susan and I went to visit them. I held the baby in my arms and silently blessed her in the name of the Father, Son and Holy Spirit and prayed that she would come to know Jesus Christ as her personal Saviour and Lord. I did not mention this to my sister.

As 1998 unfolded, disheartened, I had given up on my sister but the Lord was working his purposes out. On a Saturday morning in mid-May I attended a leadership course at my church. There was a teaching session on the gift of prophecy and during the last 30 minutes we split into small groups. We had hardly sat down when one woman said "I see a woman in Arab dress and the Lord is saying that he will take away the veil from her face so that she can see". I broke down as I knew that was my sister.

My Years Of Praying Answered

It was six weeks later on 8th July that my sister and the baby came to stay. That afternoon the sun was shining so the three of us, Salima in the pushchair, went for a walk alongside the river and as we walked I explained that I had recently been to a funeral where a well-known Christian leader had spoken. Miriam piped up that she knew him from watching television, which amazed me. Then as soon as we sat on the bench, she broke down and said "I've had enough of this control and I'm missing Jesus". I was both overjoyed and shocked but concerned for the safety of herself and the baby. I told her to keep her faith secret from her husband as I believed there could be harmful consequences if he found out. She kept silent for two weeks.

One day at work I mentioned to a colleague that I felt my sister had revealed her secret to her husband. On arriving home I mentioned the same thing to my wife, and the phone immediately rang. It was my sister telling me what I had suspected. I advised her to quickly pack a suitcase and together with her baby to come and stay with us for her protection.

During the week she stayed with us we went together to a prayer group where she related how she had wanted to visit the town when my wife and I were at work. As she walked through the porch she muttered to herself "where is my scarf", and as she walked down the High Street she felt everyone looking at her. The prayer group leader asked her whether she had been set free from the spirit of Islam and whether she wanted to be. She readily accepted and was set free. This was so crucial for the coming battle when she went back to London to "face the music".

On hearing she had become a Christian most of her Muslim friends ostracised her, one even sending a "poison pen" letter in which she stated that "she had betrayed Islam". (Miriam now worships in a church where this woman's parents are actively involved). Stephen tried his best to convince her of "the error of her ways" as he saw what she had done as a personal betrayal. On one occasion he said that he was not surprised that she had become a Christian as he had been having dreams about her. He said that he saw her surrounded by a wall of fire, and he knew that she was in hell for being an apostate. She rang me and I told her that Stephen was right about the wall of fire but wrong about the interpretation, as the prophet Zachariah (Zachariah 2:5) says that this is God's protection for his people.

After fifteen months Miriam and her daughter were able to leave London and come and live near us and they are now settled into the church community, school and neighbourhood. The only missing person in this family is Stephen who we pray will come to know Jesus Christ as his personal Saviour and Lord and come home to his family. Salima has been praying for him even though she has not seen him since she was six months old.

Dawah Or Muslim Missionary Activity

Islam has many full time missionaries in the West and elsewhere in the world, whose main task is to promote Islam and win converts. Many of these missionaries are living by faith. In the aftermath of 9/11, Muslims have been holding meetings in churches throughout the UK to explain Islam to Christians, and this is still continuing. It was only a short while ago that my husband walked into a church hall in a town in rural England and found to his amazement a combined churches meeting on Islam. He was not the speaker;

Some people convert to Islam because in their loneliness they are befriended by a Muslim.

the meeting was being led by white British converts to Islam. The elderly man who led the meeting spoke softly in glowing terms about how Islam was a religion of peace and how wonderful it was. The young girls who accompanied him looked attractive in their smart dress with the hijab. It is part of their missionary strategy to present Islam in very appealing ways. What they emphasise is Islam as a religion of peace, and they describe how Islam and Christianity have so much in common.

Some people convert to Islam because in their loneliness they are befriended by a Muslim. Muslims call this dawah, meaning Muslim evangelism or mission. It can happen in many situations, but significant numbers of young people are becoming Muslims in British universities, where there are now nearly always Muslim groups similar to Christian Unions. These groups can often be radical; and have an agenda for dawah actively seek converts.

There is a story of a young black man who converted to Islam and was radicalised through one of these groups at university. One day he felt compelled to follow a Christian man he knew, who led him to a prayer meeting in a church. As soon as he entered the church he saw a small group of about 15 people at prayer, and the leader of the group called out to him "Why are you sinning against God?" The Holy Spirit fell on the man and he had a dramatic conversion to Christ.

All over the world Christian girls are being targeted by Muslim men.

A group of girls from one Christian Union in a sixth form college wrote to us saying that they were now meeting with the Muslim group in the university in combined meetings. "Wasn't it wonderful," they said. We were alarmed, knowing that the purpose of the Muslim group would be dawah and targeting the girls for marriage.

In Islam it is permissible for a Muslim man to marry a Christian or Jewish girl. In fact it is encouraged as it is a legitimate means of dawah and brings the blessing of Allah. All over the world Christian girls are being targeted by Muslim men. Middle Eastern men who are very wealthy come to Britain to find western girls. They appear romantic, passionate and intelligent, and woo women by wining and dining. However it is not permissible for a Muslim girl to marry a Christian or Jewish boy.

Women Convert By Reading The Qur'an And Becoming Involved In Islam

There are other reasons why women convert to Islam. One is through the reading of the Qur'an; some modern English versions of the Qur'an are specially designed to give a rosy picture of Islam. It is not until after conversion that the women become fully aware of the nature of the religion they have embraced.

At university, studies in Arabic, the Middle East and similar subjects can result in women converting to Islam. As they travel to the Middle East for part of the course they can be targeted for marriage by Muslim men or can become involved with Islam as an extension of their course.

5

CULTURAL AND RELIGIOUS DIFFERENCES BETWEEN ISLAM AND THE WEST

Different Attitudes To The Sexes

Yasmin was excited. She had just arrived at the hospital as the baby was on its way. She was sure that she was carrying a boy as she had been praying so hard to Allah and she really had the feeling that it was a boy. Everyone had been telling her that it was a boy. She felt so happy. Her husband, accompanying her to the hospital, was looking forward in such anticipation to the birth. He would sit there and wait until his son had arrived. It could be a long wait, but he would sit quietly in the waiting room while Yasmin gave birth. He wouldn't go in and see her because that was women's business. He was thinking … everyone would congratulate him and come and see him, he would have a new status, a new importance.

Suddenly the baby had come. The midwife resounded, "You have a lovely baby girl!" Fear gripped Yasmin's heart; she must have heard wrongly. "What did you say?" The midwife repeated herself, "It's a beautiful girl". Suddenly Yasmin felt sick. How would she tell her husband, what would he say? He would be ashamed, and would despise her. She had produced a girl – a girl when she was so sure that it was a boy. Of course it was her fault; maybe she hadn't prayed enough. Suddenly the world was a different place and she became full of fear.

In Islam, when a girl is born it is considered the deficiency of the mother, even though medical evidence proves otherwise. Condolences are offered to the father, like at a funeral, and the midwife might say to the mother, "well next time". In some countries the midwife has been known to slap the mother after the birth, as the girl has brought shame to the family. As a result of this shame the birth will often go unannounced.

When a Muslim marries and has children, boys are always preferred. Why is this? It is because boys stay with the family and so increase the economic wealth, while girls leave home and go to live with their in-laws. A girl is a liability because she will have to be given a dowry when she

In Islam, when a girl is born it is considered the deficiency of the mother, even though medical evidence proves otherwise.

marries, while a son will bring a wife into the family, which brings status and honour and pride of place in the community. It is considered imperative that boys are produced, both for the continuity of the family and for the parents' survival into old age. Therefore if only girls are born it can cause a wife great anguish and severe stress, which puts strain on the marriage.

I recently heard of a Muslim woman in New Zealand who on producing a girl was severely beaten by her husband. The husband was told by the authorities that this behaviour was unacceptable in New Zealand and would not be tolerated.

However it is difficult to know what is happening behind the scenes with this family, as the wife who previously had helped in the shop now never appears in public. Events have taken a tragic turn for her as she has just produced another girl.

Relationships Between The Sexes

In Muslim culture, relationships between the sexes are totally different from those in western culture. Women in Islamic communities ideally only speak to women apart from male relatives, and the men in theory only speak to men apart from female members of their own household. This has implications in that Islamic culture does not permit casual friendships across the sexes as we have in western countries. Therefore a girl married to a Muslim would have difficulty even speaking to, let alone having a long conversation with a man who wasn't a relative. It would be totally alien to the cultural norms of the society, and would promote jealousy and suspicion within the marriage. It would also bring shame for the family within the community. In traditional Islamic societies all relationships are either based on the family or on keeping to same sex relationships.

...Islamic culture does not permit casual friendships across the sexes as we have in western countries.

Honour And Shame

In many areas Muslims don't think in terms of right versus wrong, but instead think in terms of honour versus shame. It can be very difficult for us to understand a society that does not have accepted ideas of right or wrong, but instead is founded on a completely different worldview. This is particularly hard for us to comprehend as Christians, as we are taught what is right and wrong as a fundamental part of Christian doctrine. Christians believe that what is wrong is sin before God, and we are commanded to be holy as Christ was holy.

One of the most important concepts in Islamic culture is that of family honour, or *izzat*. People's behaviour must be guided by the aim of not bringing shame on the family. If a member of the family is responsible for any wrongdoing or if they are in any circumstances that could be conceived as shameful, it must be kept within the family circle and hidden from the outside world. The honour of the family must be maintained at all costs. This is pivotal in the life of any Muslim family.

For example, if a Muslim girl was engaged and then decided to break it off, the family would feel that she had brought shame to them. In these circumstances many western parents might be thankful that their daughter had not married the wrong man and ended up in an unhappy marriage. But in Muslim culture, the fact that the girl felt she couldn't go through with the marriage for whatever reason would not be acceptable, and the likelihood that the marriage would have been unhappy is irrelevant. Likewise if a wife has an affair, or is even perceived by the man or his relatives to be having an affair, she brings

In Muslim societies the fear of bringing shame is used as the controlling force in people's lives, and as a result people do not have the freedom to act as they want.

shame on the family. Shame is paramount.

In Muslim societies the fear of bringing shame is used as the controlling force in people's lives, and as a result people do not have the freedom to act as they want. They must always act honourably so the honour of the family can be upheld at all times. This may mean, for example, that a married woman is not free to go out alone, work, or talk to men as people will think she is flirting, or having an affair and this will shame her family. These are tensions that someone who marries a Muslim must take into consideration as she will have to adhere to these cultural concepts.

Sexual control of women is seen as necessary within Islam, so dress becomes important and must be modest. In most Muslim communities the woman must be well covered. Wearing short skirts, jeans or clothing that is too tight is considered immoral and brings shame on the family. The woman's shame would cause the men of her family shame too, since it implies that her male relatives were too weak to control her.

the Muslim family's priority is to educate the males in the family.

Muslims girls are expected to remain virgins until they get married, otherwise they will be considered damaged property. In Tunisia a European woman was working as a waitress in a hotel where she met a Tunisian man, fell in love with him, and went to live with him. He wanted to marry her but said that she first had to convert to Islam. She refused. After one year he became very religious and told her that his parents wanted him to marry a virgin. Because they had lived together and not married, his parents felt she had lost her honour and they could never trust her.

It is common for Muslim girls to leave school at sixteen and stay at home to do the family cooking and cleaning until they marry. Many are not allowed to go to university or have any further education. Their parents see this as being for the girl's own good: she will be protected, no harm will come to her and she will be pure and a virgin when she gets married. The ultimate shame is producing a child outside of marriage. This excessive zeal with which girls must be guarded and their virginity protected makes them an almost intolerable burden on the family. Therefore husbands will be found for them and they will be handed over to their in-laws as soon as possible. Further education is not generally seen as essential for girls; the Muslim family's priority is to educate the males in the family.

One family told me that if their daughter was beaten by her husband they would do nothing about it as it would bring shame on the entire family. They would rather keep their honour and let their daughter suffer. As long as it was hidden from the outside world that would satisfy them.

Honour Killings

The meaning of Islam is "submission", or "to conform". If someone refuses to conform he is acting shamefully. An old Arab proverb says a concealed shame is two thirds forgiven. One way shame can be eliminated is by revenge or honour killing. If a wife is

One way shame can be eliminated is by revenge or honour killing.

having, or even suspected of having an affair, the husband and family can kill her to maintain their honour. In many Muslim countries this is perfectly acceptable and the authorities turn a blind eye. In Pakistan and other countries this is being abused further, as husbands who want to get rid of their wives use the excuse of honour killings. There are hundreds of honour killings very year in India and Pakistan and we are now seeing a number in the West.

An acquaintance of mine was having beauty treatment at Harrods in London. She started a conversation with a woman next to her, also having beauty treatment, from a Middle Eastern country. The woman had just returned to Britain after spending some time with her family and told her that while she was there her sister was found to be having an affair. This brought shame on the family and to restore their honour the family had to take her outside and stone her. She took half an hour to die. The next day this woman was sitting in Harrods speaking of it as though it was a normal event in her life.

> **There is a grey area between yes and no. No is not as definitive as we might expect it to be.**

Another story comes out of the Middle East of a mother of two children having an affair. The extended family stoned the mother to death insisting that the children watch their mother die. The man she had an affair with was also killed.

Lying Or Taqiyya

In Islam there is not such a condemnation of lying as there

is in western culture, and there are references in various hadith.(sayings attributed to the Muslim prophet Muhammad) that allow it. It is permissible to lie in three situations: in war for the benefit of Islam; in reconciliation between two people who have quarrelled; and to your women. Therefore it is considered permissible to lie in order to marry a person who will be converted to Islam. Also a man is allowed to lie to his wife.

There is a grey area between yes and no. No is not as definitive as we might expect it to be. Yes can mean no and no can mean yes. I remember the time when I invited a Muslim family to a church barbecue, and they told me that they would definitely come. However they were only saying that to please and they actually had no intention of coming.

Polygamy

It says in the Qur'an that a man can have up to four wives at one time. (sura 4:3)

> ....*marry of the women who seem good to you, two or three or four...*

Many people ask if this really happens in the West. Do Muslim men here take more than one wife? The answer is yes; Muslim men do have more than one wife in western countries. But how can this happen and it not be called polygamy and against the law of the country. The second marriage takes place with only a religious ceremony at a mosque that is not registered for civil marriage (for example only 160 mosques in Britain out of 1500 are registered for civil marriage). The marriage is conducted under Shariah Law which has enormous implications if the marriage fails.

Or the husband might simply make a visit to his country of origin and marry another woman but not bring her to the western country where he lives. He will leave the new wife there and visit her from time to time.

However many women who marry Muslims do not live in western countries but in the husband's country of origin where, in the majority of cases, polygamy is permitted. It certainly must be noted that if you marry a Muslim man the possibility of polygamy is always there, even if it seems an impossibility at this moment and even if he says he will never do it.

Polygamy causes great hardship to women with jealousies, quarrels, competition and humiliation developing between the wives and children. It is also discriminatory against the woman to the benefit of the man and can cause great pain and agony. In marrying a Muslim it can always be a worry that the husband

It certainly must be noted that if you marry a Muslim man the possibility of polygamy is always there, even if it seems an impossibility at this moment and even if he says he will never do it.

might want to take another wife. In the majority of cases it won't happen but there are cases where it does and it is all too easy to say, "This could never happen to me". One English woman married to a Muslim found she was facing exactly this situation. When the couple were struggling with marriage difficulties they consulted a very well known Muslim leader for counselling, and his recommendation was that her husband should take another wife.

When I was in south East Asia a while ago I visited a friend who worked in a girls' secondary school, where she had arranged for me to speak to some of the Muslim women teachers. It was quite an eye-opener, as I heard intelligent,

At the beginning so many women are unaware of all the implications and complications that lie under the surface

well-educated women saying things that were amazing to me. One woman I talked with said that if her husband wanted to take a second wife she would just have to accept it. She felt she had no choice in the matter; it was up to him. At a later date my friend told me that this woman's husband had indeed recently taken another wife, and the pain and heartache that it was causing the teacher was unimaginable. She was barely coping.

In the Qur'an it says that a wife should be consulted before the husband takes a second wife. However in practice this is not usually the case and the husband will generally just go ahead and find one. The first wife is then presented with this new woman. In one country of south East Asia there is a lot of controversy and debate about this. Some say that for Islam to be credible in this area the first wife must be consulted and must agree. In Tunisia polygamy is not permitted.

On the face of it, embracing Islam can seem so straightforward, whether you enter it by marriage, conviction or otherwise. At the beginning so many women are unaware of all the implications and complications that lie under the surface.

6

WHAT DOES ISLAM SAY ABOUT WOMEN

East Meets West

Western culture and Islamic culture, Christianity and Islam are completely different world views which in various aspects are diametrically opposed. We see this in a range of issues from the position of women in Islam to children and divorce.

The Qur'an And Hadith

Islamic teaching comes not only from the Qur'an but also from the Hadith. The Hadith, or traditions, is a collection of words and deeds of Muhammad. It must be noted that the words of the Hadith are not always the words of Muhammad but how the people around him understood them, or what people were saying or doing at that time. There is also the difficulty of the authenticity of the tradition whether it is strong, weak or forged.

> **Western culture and Islamic culture, Christianity and Islam are completely different world views which in various aspects are diametrically opposed.**

When the Qur'an and traditions do not say anything about a particular subject, rules are drawn up by consensus of the religious leaders (*ijma*) and by analogous reasoning (*qiyas*). The combination of the Qur'an, Hadith, *ijma* and *qiyas* were used by Islamic scholars to create the body of rules and regulations known as the Shariah or Islamic Law.

Do Women Have Equality In Islam

Men and women are not equal in Islam. Islam limits a woman's role to her biology or to the home. Therefore many Muslim women say that because of these preconceptions she is very limited in what she can do. The values that Islam has attributed to women are those of being weak, inferior, inherently evil, intellectually incapable and spiritually lacking. The result of this is that Muslim men see women in a different light from western men and behave in different ways.

Men's Superiority In Islam

The Qur'an says:

> *Men have authority over women because Allah has made the one superior to the other.*

(4:34 Qur'an transl by N.J.Dawood)

Men are considered superior to women in Islam and this is reflected in family life, where the oldest male member of the family has the position of authority within the family and controls family life. If you remember Mary's story, as soon

The Qur'an says: "Men have authority over women because Allah has made the one superior to the other."

as her husband arrived in Britain he began to exercise his authority and that authority was absolute. Any contradiction meant arguments and violence. He also did exactly what he wanted without mentioning it to his wife. This would be the normal pattern.

In Muslim culture there is no sharing of household duties, no changing of nappies by men as is now expected in the West, as this is considered a woman's job. There are definite boundaries around the areas of activity expected of the sexes, and no flexibility. Having said this, there are Muslim women who do rise above the limited expectations placed on them, but these are generally educated, go-ahead women who are indomitable and strong in spirit. The majority succumb to a life of abuse and hardship, where ill treatment is the norm.

Women in Islam do not have equal rights to men. It is difficult for non-Muslims and even Muslims to bring this subject for discussion in the public arena as it means disclosing secrets behind the image of the traditional Muslim family which would bring shame. In fact the position of women in Islam is a human rights issue which needs to be addressed.

A Woman's Destiny

In the Hadith (301:1 Bukhari) it says:

> Once Allah's Apostle said to a group of women, "Give alms, as I have seen that the majority of the dwellers of Hell-fire were you (women)."…I have not seen anyone more deficient in intelligence and religion than you. A cautious sensible man could be led astray by some of you." The women asked, "O Allah's Apostle! What is deficient in our intelligence and religion?" He said, "Is not the evidence of two women equal to the witness of one man?" They replied in the affirmative. He said, "This is the deficiency in your intelligence. Isn't it true that a woman can neither pray nor fast during her menses?"

The verse above states that most of the people in hell are women. So how does a woman get into paradise? The answer, spelled out elsewhere in the Hadith, is that a wife has to be absolutely obedient to her husband. It is this that shows her piety and guarantees her eternal destiny. He is her paradise or her hell; without obedience to her

Women in paradise must be submissive, subordinate, veiled and secluded in the harems of heaven, watching quietly as their husbands make love with the beautiful houris (perpetual virgins) of paradise.

husband there is no heaven for a woman. The husband is so elevated compared to the woman that he is placed on a divine level.

The wives of the righteous and obedient are mentioned as accompanying their husbands in paradise. Women in paradise must be submissive, subordinate, veiled and secluded in the harems of heaven, watching quietly as their husbands make love with the beautiful houris (perpetual virgins) of paradise. Man is her master on earth, and she will be subjugated to him forever in heaven as well.

Women Considered Deficient In Intelligence

The Hadith quoted above states that women are considered deficient in intelligence, as well as in religion. One reason given is that a woman's brain is considered smaller than the man's. Amin Qasim, a male feminist Muslim writer has said that if men are superior to women in both physical strength and intelligence it is because men were engaged in work activities that required them to use their brains and bodies and therefore to develop them. Women who have been deprived of all opportunity to use mind or body are forced into an inferior position.

An eminent Arabic writer named Al-'Aqad says that a woman's share of intellect does not reach a man's level, and goes on to demolish the idea of the intellectual equality of men and women. This seems to be a well-established view that has lasted over the centuries that women are not as intelligent as men.

Discipline Of Women: Wife Beating Permitted

The Qur'an (4:34) says:

> So good women are the obedient, guarding in secret that which Allah hath guarded. As for those from whom you fear rebellion, admonish them, and banish them to beds apart and scourge them. Then if they obey you, seek not a way against them.

The above verse was revealed in connection with a woman who complained to Muhammad that her husband slapped her on the face (which was still marked with the slap). At first Muhammad told her to get even with him, and then added, "Wait until I think about it." Later on, the above verse was revealed after which Muhammad said, "We wanted one thing but Allah wanted another, and what Allah wanted is best."

If a woman refuses to sleep with her husband or does not obey his command, she will be admonished first, and later the man is permitted by Allah to beat his wife.

This verse permits wife beating. The man has a responsibility to admonish his wife, the right to desert her sexually by moving into a separate bed, and the right to beat her to correct any rebelliousness in behaviour. The word "rebellion" here refers to any disobedience on the part of the woman, not simply a refusal to engage in sex. If a woman refuses to sleep with her husband or does not obey his command, she will be admonished first, and later the man is permitted by Allah to beat his wife.

The wife of a Muslim should always be ready to come to bed and satisfy her husband's sexual desires, otherwise she may be beaten by him and cursed by the angels of Allah, who are commissioned to have a close watch over the sexual affairs of a couple. Muhammad is quoted as saying that if a man invites his wife to sleep with him and she refuses to come to him, then the angels send their curses on her until morning (Hadith 121:7 Bukhari). A man's sexual desires are considered so urgent that it is better to let food burn in the oven than let a man's desires remain unfulfilled.

As one Muslim scholar put it "There is wickedness and weakness in women. Diplomacy and harshness is the remedy for wickedness and gentleness is the remedy for weakness"

Women Deficient As Witnesses

In the Qur'an (2:282) it says:

And call to witness, from among your men, two witnesses. And if two men be not (at hand) then a man and two women of such as ye approve as witnesses, so that if the one erreth (through forgetfulness) the other will remember.

From this Muslim jurists have firmly asserted that it is divine intervention that one male witness is equal to two women witnesses. They also assert that the witness given by two women will be valid only when accompanied by a man. If two male witnesses are not available then there should be one man and two women, not four women. Four women cannot replace two men.

Rape

In countries like Pakistan a woman who is raped has to produce four adult Muslim male witnesses who have seen the act take place. If she can't she will then be charged with adultery, sentenced to prison and given a number of lashes. This is the situation of women in countries where the law of the country follows Shariah on this particular issue.

Inheritance

In the Qur'an (sura 4:11) it says:

> Allah chargeth you concerning (the provision for) your children: to the male the equivalent of the portion of two females.

In Shariah Law women do not have equal inheritance to men and only get half share of the male heirs.

In Britain, Muslim husbands are going to specialist Shariah lawyers who will advise on the drawing up of Shariah compliant wills. This means that the wife will only inherit a part of her share of the inheritance.

In Shariah Law women do not have equal inheritance to men and only get half share of the male heirs.

Divorce

Divorce can take place very easily in Islam and the power of divorce resides in the hands of the man. It is not considered shameful for a man to divorce a wife, whatever the reason, though it is considered very shameful for a woman to initiate a divorce and it will affect the whole extended family. In Islamic countries where there is Shariah Law the man has only to say "I divorce you" three times, and

It is a very common custom in Muslim societies for the man to threaten divorce without really intending to go through with it.

that constitutes the divorce. After divorce the children are considered the property of the father.

It is a very common custom in Muslim societies for the man to threaten divorce without really intending to go through with it. This is a means of keeping his wife under control. Many women marrying Muslims in Britain are married in mosques that are not registered for marriage with no accompanying civil ceremony. They are therefore not married according to British Law but are under Shariah Law. This means that if the relationship breaks down, only Shariah Law is implemented and there is no legal divorce procedure. This is to the woman's detriment in cases of divorce and also bereavement as she will not be legally entitled to receive a spouse's share of the assets.

After divorce, some Muslim men kidnap the children and return to their country of origin. Many of these countries do not have any agreement with western countries for access to children and the woman ends up losing her children. There are thousands of western women in this predicament worldwide and it is causing enormous emotional pain. In the best cases a woman might see her children about twice a year; in the worst case scenario she will never see her children again and never know their whereabouts. Women in this situation often spend large amounts of money trying to trace their children, and endure untold pain and suffering. They might have to fight the legal system of that country, which would most likely be shaped by Islamic thinking, culture and law, all of which fall heavily on the side of the husband. He of course was aware of this when he married the woman, whereas she could probably never have dreamed her marriage would turn out this way.

A marriage across cultures and religions can be very difficult and have far reaching implications for the children.

Children

When a western woman marries a Muslim the children will always be brought up as Muslims and will have to attend Islamic teaching at the mosque after school. A Muslim man does not have to accept children from a previous marriage if he considers the children will take up too much of their mother's time.

Many years ago a British woman, who is now a Christian, married a Pakistani barrister in Britain and converted to Islam on marriage. Even though she is now a Christian they remain married. They had four daughters who turned out to be very different from one another. As they grew up the girls were taught about Islam. One of the daughters became a Muslim and follows the religion very closely. A younger daughter became a born again Christian and is involved in Christian music and worship, sharing Christ with others and praying for her family. There is a very wide gulf between these two sisters, which has brought tension and conflict between them. The Christian sister has often tried to share her faith and the Gospel with her sister, while her sister has always jumped to defend Islam and her Islamic practice and belief.

As these children grow up they may well experience a crisis as they search for an identity of their own.

A marriage across cultures and religions can be very difficult and have far reaching implications for the children. A third daughter of this family lives with an English man as her partner but has not married him. When the Christian daughter became engaged to a fellow Christian, she discussed the marriage with her father and asked him to come to the wedding and give her away. The father has found both of these situations very difficult and was quite resistant at first to attending the wedding. However in the end he did take part in the wedding and gave his daughter away.

In the movie East is East, a Pakistani man marries an English woman in the early 1960s and as the children grow up he expects them to conform to the norms and traditions of their Muslim upbringing. When the children begin to rebel and do not live up to his expectations he finds it very difficult to understand and cope with, and this creates a huge conflict within the family. Many Muslim men in similar situations become very oppressive and abusive towards their children.

The Question Of Identity

One difficulty in these marriages is the conflict of identity. Within a Muslim family living in the West there may be severe cultural conflicts as daughters growing up in the West want a life similar to their western friends. The family, on the other hand, wants them to behave in the traditional way, as they would if they were living in their country of origin. But in the story above there is a religious conflict between family members, as well as a cultural conflict. These are two worlds that the children cannot bridge as they are so entirely different in their nature, practice and expectations.

As these children grow up they may well experience a crisis as they search for an identity of their own. Some find it in fundamentalist Muslim groups, where the idea of the worldwide community of Muslims, the *umma*, draws them to political allegiances with fellow Muslims in places liked Palestine and Afghanistan.

7

WHAT HAPPENS WHEN A PERSON LEAVES ISLAM

It is said that Islam is a one way street; you can enter it but you cannot leave.

The Apostasy Law

Islamic religious law (Shariah) states that Muslim men who convert to another faith (apostates) and refuse to return to Islam should be put to death. It also specifies various other penalties including the annulment of their marriage, the loss of their children and all their property, and the suspension of all financial and legal contracts and inheritance rights. All are to be returned if they revert to Islam.

There are four principal schools of Shariah within Sunni Islam and a fifth tradition within Shi'a Islam. There is some disagreement as to the detailed application of apostasy law between the Islamic scholars from the different traditions. One question in dispute between the traditions is whether female apostates should be executed as well, or just imprisoned for life, and whether children of converts should also be considered apostates. However all schools of Shariah agree that adult male apostates who refuse to return to Islam should be executed and that their Muslim wife and children and all their property should be taken away from them.

Remember Miriam, who told her story in chapter 4, was considered an apostate by her friends and husband when she converted to Christianity. Stephen was advised that as she had become a Christian she was to be regarded as an apostate and therefore the marriage was null and void. He was therefore ordered to leave the house immediately. Miriam had only been married by Shariah, with no civil ceremony, so as soon as she became a Christian the marriage was automatically annulled.

In the year 2000 a young Muslim woman converted to Christianity in Britain. One day she was snatched from outside her church and bundled into a van by several people who included some of her own relatives. As the van sped away she was beaten badly. She was given a copy of the Qur'an and ordered to recite the Islamic creed in an attempt to force her to return to Islam. She refused and began to sing the Christian song, "My Jesus, my Saviour there is none like you". The beatings continued. Eventually she was dumped from the van in front of a shopping centre, from where she was taken to hospital. When she recovered she had to go into hiding.

...all schools of Shariah agree that adult male apostates who refuse to return to Islam should be executed and that their Muslim wife and children and all their property should be taken away from them.

Converts are often rejected by their families and thrown out of the family home. In Pakistan all the members of a wealthy Muslim family converted to Christianity in 2001. The husband's extended family seized their comfortable home, as they had become apostates. As a consequence of their conversion the family had to give up their affluent lifestyle and go into hiding.

Even in the most tolerant Muslim nations where there is no law of apostasy and the state does not arrest or punish converts, Muslims who convert to another faith can face enormous social pressure from their families and communities. This can be a major problem even in western countries with Muslim minority communities. In these situations their lives may not be in danger, but other Shariah-prescribed penalties for conversion, such as attempts to force them to return to Islam, forced separation from their spouse, and the loss of children and property may be forced upon them by the family and community.

> **Converts are often rejected by their families and thrown out of the family home.**

Yasmin's Story

Yasmin was brought up in a Muslim family. She converted after having a vision of Jesus when she gave birth to her youngest son, and was baptised in her thirties. "My family completely disowned me. They thought I had committed the biggest sin, as I was born a Muslim so I must die a Muslim. When my husband found out, he totally disowned my sons. One friend tried to strangle me when I told him I was converting," she said.

"We had bricks through our windows. I was spat at in the street because they thought I was dishonouring Islam. We had to call the police so many times. I had to go to court to get an injunction against my husband because he was inciting others to attack me."

She fled to another part of Britain, but the attacks soon started again as locals found out about her. "I wasn't going to leave again," she said, adding that it was the double standards of her attackers that made her most angry. "They are such hypocrites - they want us to be tolerant of everything they want, but they are intolerant of everything about us."

With other converts, Yasmin has helped to set up a series of support groups across England, which has adopted a method of operating, normally associated with dictatorships, not democracies. They not only have to meet in secret, but they cannot advertise their services and have to vet those that approach them to make sure they are not infiltrators.

> I was spat at in the street because they thought I was dishonouring Islam.

Yasmin says that she is in contact with about 70 converts. Some of these have been beaten "black and blue" for their faith, others suffer even more. The family of an 18 year-old girl whom Yasmin was helping found that she had been hiding a Bible in her room and visiting church secretly. "I tried to do as much as possible to help her, but they took her to Pakistan 'on holiday'", Yasmin recounts. "Three weeks later, she was drowned. They said that she went out in the middle of the night and slipped into the river, but she just wouldn't have done that."

Ruth's Story

Ruth, also of Pakistani origin, found out recently that she had only just escaped being murdered. When she told her family that she had converted, they kept her locked inside the family home all summer.

"They were afraid I would meet some Christians. My brother was aggressive, and even hit me. I later found out he wanted me dead," she said. A family friend had suggested taking her to Pakistan to kill her, and her brother put the idea to her mother, who ruled against it. "You are very isolated and very alone. But now, my brother is thinking about changing and a cousin has made a commitment to Christianity."

Noor's Story

Noor, from the Midlands, was brought up a Muslim but converted to Christianity at twenty-one. "Telling my father was the most difficult thing I have ever done. I thought he would kill me on the spot, but he just went into a state of shock," she said. He ended up almost kidnapping her.

"He took drastic action; he took the family to Pakistan, to a secluded village with no roads to it. He kept us there for many years, putting pressure on me to leave my Christian faith. I endured mental and emotional suffering that most humans never reach," she said.

"In desperation, my father threatened to take my life. If someone converts, it is a must for family honour to bring them back to Islam, or if not, to kill them."

them back to Islam, or if not, to kill them." Eventually, her father realised that he could not shake her faith,

Even the most liberal Muslim can become incredibly fierce if you criticise Islam, or, horror of horrors, leave it."

and released her with strict conditions.

Imams in Britain sometimes call on apostates to be killed if they criticise their former religion. Anwar Sheikh, a former mosque teacher from Pakistan, became an atheist after coming to Britain. He now lives with a special alarm in his house in Cardiff, after criticising Islam in a series of hardline books.

"I've had 18 fatwas against me. They telephone me – they aren't foolhardy enough to put it in writing. I had a call a couple of weeks ago. They mean repent or be hanged," he said. "What I have written, I believe and I will not take it back. I will suffer the consequences. If that is the price, I will pay it."

The most high-profile British apostate is Ibn Warraq, a Pakistani-born intellectual and former teacher from London who lost his faith after the Salman Rushdie affair and set out his reasons in the book *Why I am not a Muslim*. He recently edited the book *Leaving Islam*, but finds it hard to explain the hostility. "It's very strange. Even the most liberal Muslim can become incredibly fierce if you criticise Islam, or, horror of horrors, leave it."

He himself has taken the precaution of using only a pseudonym, and lives incognito in mainland Europe. He thinks that Islamic apostasy is common. "In Western societies, it is probably 10-15 per cent. It's very difficult to tell, because people don't admit it."

8

WHAT DO MUSLIMS BELIEVE?

T he word Islam means "submission to Allah" and the Muslim is the one who submits.

The Qur'an

The Qur'an is the holy book of Islam and is said to have existed eternally in heaven in Arabic on tablets of stone. Speakers of Arabic have a special prestige in the eyes of the Muslim world. Muslims believe that the Qur'an is the actual word of God, dictated word by word to Muhammad in the last 23 years of his life by the angel Gabriel, in Arabic. They believe that it is not possible to translate it into other languages.

The Qur'an is the same length as the New Testament and is divided into 114 suras or chapters. However the suras are not arranged in chronological order but roughly in order of length, starting with the longest and ending with the shortest. It is necessary to know the context of the sura, and when and where they were revealed. Many verses in the Qur'an appear contradictory and this

Many people find the Qur'an very difficult to read, as it is not possible to pick it up and immediately understand it as we do the Bible.

is resolved by the "doctrine of abrogation" whereby the later revelation will abrogate, or cancel, the earlier revelation. Many people find the Qur'an very difficult to read, as it is not possible to pick it up and immediately understand it as we do the Bible.

The first sura of the Qur'an has only seven verses and is the main Muslim prayer with which they start every prayer and every prostration. The Qur'an is read in conjunction with the second sacred book the Hadith, which is thousands of Muhammad's sayings and deeds collected by his companions from 275 to 350 years after his death.

Muslims believe that the Qur'an is the final revelation of God and it superseded all earlier revelations including the Bible.

The Five Pillars Of Islam

Muslims have a set of religious duties called the five pillars of Islam. These are very simple and are compulsory for every Muslim.

The Confession Or The Creed

The Muslim's confession of faith is the first pillar of Islam and is called the *shahada*. It is: "I bear witness and testify there is no god but God (Allah) and Muhammad is the messenger of God (Allah)." This is the Islamic creed and is repeated daily in the round of required prayers. When this is recited by non-Muslims in the presence of two witnesses a person becomes a Muslim. In cases of forced conversion, the person is forced to recite the *shahada* and they are then considered to have converted to Islam. When a baby is born the Imam recites this *shahada* in the baby's ear. The *shahada* is literally proclaimed from the rooftops in Muslim countries, as it is part of the call to prayer by the muezzin from the minaret. What in effect is being proclaimed from the rooftops is a denial of the sonship and the deity of Christ.

Prayer

The second pillar of Islam is prayer. Muslims pray five times a day at set times facing towards Mecca. The times of prayers are the dawn prayer before sunrise, the noon prayer, the late afternoon prayer, the prayer immediately after the sun sets and the prayer after nightfall. The Qur'an gives no details of this, as it is all to be found in the Hadith. The ritual movements from standing to kneeling to prostration were all part of pagan Arabic culture before Islam.

What in effect is being proclaimed from the rooftops is a denial of the sonship and the deity of Christ.

Prayer at a mosque is announced by the call to prayer from high on the minaret five times a day. The muezzin cries, "Allah is great. I confess there is no God but Allah. I testify that Muhammad is the messenger of Allah. Come to prayer, come to do good (success)". Early in the morning he calls "Prayer is better than sleep. Allah is great..."

Before prayer the Muslim must carry out a prescribed ceremonial washing called ablutions. There are rules for washing four parts of the body: the face, from the top of the forehead to the chin and as far as each ear; the hands and arms, up to the elbows; a fourth part of the head is rubbed with the wet hand; and the feet are washed up to the ankles.

Many Muslims believe that if any of these parts of the body are not washed all the ritual prayers made afterwards are of no value. The Muslim should also be sober and ritually pure from sexual pollution.

After having performed the ablutions the worshipper then proceeds to the recitation of the prescribed prayers accompanied by ritual movements. This can be done in either private or public, and it is common in some countries to see Muslim men doing their prayers on the street. In Britain more and more work places, schools, universities, and prisons are providing prayer rooms as Muslims ask for them. Airports and hospitals have multi-faith prayer rooms which can prove difficult in some cases as Muslim men would object to praying in a room that had women present with their shoes on and their heads uncovered. A friend of ours was at one of the main British airports and she went to pray in the prayer room. The Muslims present asked her to take her shoes off at the door, which she refused to do. She entered and sat down to pray in one of the chairs in the room, and immediately one of the Muslim men came over to her and tried to forcibly remove her shoes.

Apart from daily prayers there are united prayers on a Friday which all men are obliged to attend. It is during this common public worship that the Imam or leader reviews the week's spiritual life of the community and offers advice and exhortation on good deeds and moral behaviour. It is in these Friday prayers some mosques every week have prayers cursing Jews and Christians. Generally mosques have a separate room for the women to perform ablutions and pray. A very few progressive mosques would accommodate women in the main congregation, but even then in a separate place from the men. Not all mosques have places for women and so they are required to pray at home.

There is also a tradition of *du'aa* which is another form of calling upon God that could be considered as more like extemporary praying. However many of these *du'aa* traditions are only a repetition of prayers instituted by Muhammad. The more mystical experiences take place within the Sufi tradition which was developed several hundreds of years after Muhammad's death.

Islam does not expect worshippers to develop a relationship with God in prayer; it is more an act of obligatory duty. In Christianity there is a wide diversity of prayer from structured, liturgical prayer to the extemporary prayers of the charismatic movement. Prayer for the Christian is more than a series of ritual movements and set prayers, as it is built on a personal relationship between the individual and God. Christian prayer is entry into the presence of God through Jesus Christ as the mediator. Christians can pray at any time and in any circumstance and have the confidence that God hears and answers. There are many types of prayer: personal prayer, intercessory prayer when we pray for others, prayers of adoration, prayers for healing, and sacramental prayers to name a few.

"For a Christian, when the Holy Spirit has come to reside

> **Islam does not expect worshippers to develop a relationship with God in prayer; it is more an act of obligatory duty.**

in him the person cannot stop praying for the Spirit prays without ceasing in him. No matter whether he is asleep or awake, prayer is going on in his heart all the time. He may be eating or drinking, he may be resting or working- the incense of prayer will ascend spontaneously from his heart. The slightest stirring of his heart is like a voice which sings in silence and in secret to the Invisible" (St.Isaac the Syrian)

Giving Of Alms

The third pillar of Islam is the giving of alms. In Islam two terms are used for almsgiving. One is *zakat* which is the legal obligation for every Muslim, the other is *sadaqa* which are the voluntary offerings made at *Eid-ul-fitr* the annual festival at the end of Ramadan.

Every adult Muslim must give *zakat* in proportion to the property he owns, as long as he has sufficient money for his own subsistence. In Sunni Islam the rate is 2.5 percent. *Zakat* is given to the poor and needy, those in debt, travellers, those who administer the funds and recent converts to Islam. They can also be used for the "cause of Allah", a phrase that encompasses *jihad*. In Islam prayer and alms-giving are considered inseparable and it is said in Islam that alms-giving seals prayer.

Christians are not compelled to give a fixed amount, but the Bible tells them that love for God should mean they share what they have to meet the needs of those around them. Evangelicals often "tithe" their income, which means giving away 10% of it to their local church or other causes.

Fasting

The fourth pillar of Islam is fasting. Fasting takes place during the month of Ramadan every year. This is the ninth month of the Muslim calendar and the time when Muslims believe the angel Gabriel first revealed the Qur'an to Muhammad. Ramadan is announced when one trustworthy witness testifies before the authorities that the new moon has been sighted. A cloudy sky may therefore delay or prolong the fast. The Muslim era began on the 20th June 622 when according to Muslim tradition Muhammad escaped from persecution in Mecca to a place called Yathrib. This episode is called the *hijrah,* which means flight or immigration. Muhammad later changed the name from Yathrib to Madina. The Muslim calendar begins from this date, and it is a lunar calendar with only 354 days in the year. As this is 11 days shorter than the solar year the dates on which Muslim feasts fall will vary in time every year.

There is more food consumed during the month of fasting than in any other month of the year.

Muslims teach that the significance of Ramadan is that man has larger needs than bread and that his body is to be his servant and not his master. Great self discipline is shown by those Muslims who take it seriously, as they do not even swallow their saliva. Another purpose of Ramadan is to show sympathy with the poor and destitute. Fasting is defined as abstinence from food or drink, smoking and sexual intercourse during the hours between sunrise and sunset. During the month of Ramadan the family gets up early before the sun has risen and has a large meal. After the sun has set the fast is broken, often with dates, and then there is exuberant feasting every night until very late. It is said that the joy of feasting increases every night and reaches its peak on the 27th day of Ramadan which is the final day of the fast and is called the *Eid-ul-fitr*. There is more food consumed during the month of fasting than in any other month of the year.

Fasting is compulsory for the Muslim, except for young children and the mentally disabled. Those who are sick, travelling, pregnant, nursing mothers or having their period are able to postpone their fast for a later date. This change of daily habits demands a high measure of personal will-power and self-discipline, and is less difficult in countries where everyone is doing the same.

As with prayer, Christians have no prescribed way of fasting. It is still very much a ritual of the Eastern Church, where fasting takes place every Wednesday and Friday and is a vegan fast, meaning no animal or fish products are eaten. Eastern Christians also fast during Lent for 50 days and on various other days throughout the year, where fasting takes the form of no food or drink for a period of time. The person is able to choose the length of time of their fast but it is always followed by a daily Eucharist and then a vegan meal. It differs from Ramadan in that the period of time is longer and it is not followed by feasting but a simple meal.

Evangelical Christians generally decide for themselves how and when they are going to fast, and do so to devote themselves more fully to prayer. They will abstain from food but not water usually for a period of between one to three days. This fast does not include food in the evening. They try not to let anyone know they are fasting, in line with Jesus' instruction to his disciples: "When you fast, put oil on your head and wash your face, so that it will not be obvious to others that you are fasting, but only to your Father who is unseen" (Matthew 6:17-18).

The Hajj

The fifth pillar of Islam is the *hajj* or the pilgrimage to Mecca in Saudi Arabia, where Muslims perform the *hajj* rituals around the Islamic shrine, the *Ka'aba*. This takes place in the twelfth month of the Muslim calendar. The pilgrimage is obligatory once in a lifetime for those who can afford it, some traditions permitting the sending of a substitute even posthumously.

Various rituals associated with the pilgrimage are performed, some of which were adopted by Muhammad from those performed by the idol-worshipping religions of the Arabian Peninsula hundreds of years before. They include going around the *Ka'aba* seven times, as Muslims believe this is the place where Abraham offered his son Ishmael for sacrifice and then God provided a substitute animal. (It must be noted here that Christians believe that Abraham offered up his son Isaac, and not Ishmael). This pilgrimage usually has a great effect on Muslims, and on returning they are religiously revived and consider themselves new men and women. They believe that they have had all their sins washed away and some even say that they have become "born anew".

> **There is no place in Islam for the atonement of sins or redemption as we see in the work of Jesus.**

There is no place in Islam for the atonement of sins or redemption as we see in the work of Jesus. Salvation as we know it in Christianity doesn't really exist in the Muslim worldview, as a Muslim enters heaven by virtue of works: good deeds have to outweigh the bad deeds. In Christianity we receive eternal life by accepting that Jesus died for our sins and rose again for our justification. By this we can know the forgiveness of our sins and be born anew. This is not on account of anything we can do, but because of the grace of a God who loves us.

People are attracted to Islam because it is so clearly laid out with rules and regulations, leaving little room for expressions of free will, complicated debate or argument. By following these rules it is possible to know exactly where you stand within the religion, as nothing is left to chance or not covered. In some ways this can become an easy option for those who would rather not exercise their minds but are willing to simply accept the demands of the religion.

It must be remembered that it is extremely difficult within Islam to criticise or analyse the system in relation to theology and beliefs. Everything must be accepted blindly. Although there are Muslim scholars who talk about reforming Islam, they are condemned as apostates by other parts of the Muslim community. Those who are considered blasphemous, such as author Salman Rushdie, risk losing their lives.

9

WHAT CAN BE DONE?

I have been greatly worried by the number of women I have heard of who marry Muslims, and I am deeply saddened by their stories. This is the main reason for writing this book. I am hopeful that if it is read by a woman who is thinking of either marrying a Muslim or converting to Islam or both, that something in this book might cast doubts and cause her to reconsider her decision.

However, over the years I have spoken to girls who have married Muslims and converted to Islam and I have asked them what could have been done or said that would have stopped them or made them think again. Every one of them said that there was nothing: there was nothing at all that anyone could have done as they were so madly in love they were blinded to any warning signs.

So what can the parents, relatives, friends or church members do to help a woman who is planning to marry a Muslim?

1. **The first thing that can be done is to keep very close contact with the person who is in this situation and be a listening ear.** For parents this is very important, especially if you are not happy with the relationship or the actions of your daughter. What you need to do is to stand alongside them and love and

care for them. Any whiff of opposition or criticism can make them even more determined to go through with their plans. Be open and try to get them to share their true feelings about the situation, as there are usually some doubts present. Invite her boyfriend or fiancé into your home for a meal, befriend him and try to influence him. Do not hold back from speaking about your faith.

2. It is in ignorance that many women convert to Islam on marriage. Help them to understand Islam and Islamic culture, so that they can be as informed as possible when they make their decision. **Church pastors need to educate their congregations on how to understand Islam and the implications of conversion.**

3. Instead of a quick engagement and marriage, encourage the couple to have a longer engagement.

4. For women marrying Muslims it is prudent to have a pre-nuptial agreement. This will enable a woman to get a correct share of the assets in cases of divorce. We have seen earlier that even in the West many women are marrying Muslims with only a religious ceremony at a mosque (which has not been registered been marriages) so on divorce a woman would be subject to Shariah and would be in the category of co-habitation. Lawyers are also writing Shariah wills for Muslim men where the woman would have only a part share of the assets. For women living outside of the West, it is also necessary to have a pre-nuptial agreement for the purpose of getting custody of the children if there should be a divorce. Pre-nuptial agreements are becoming increasingly common in many countries.

5. Above all "pray without ceasing" and get friends to pray as well. Commit the situation to serious intercessory prayer. Pray the Word of God into the situation.

Raising Spiritual Issues After A Person Becomes A Muslim

In the western world we are often very reticent to speak about our faith. Indeed, it is said that the two subjects we never speak about are faith and politics. This is not so in the non-western world and especially in Islamic culture. Here it is normal to speak about spiritual matters, and in fact it would be abnormal not to do so. Everyday life and religion are so intertwined that for the Muslim a separation is not possible. Thus a Muslim will readily speak about his faith and expects us to do the same. As Christians, we shouldn't be shy or diffident about speaking of our faith with Muslims, but readily share what we believe, with wisdom and sensitivity. We need to speak about our faith right from the beginning.

Can we ask Muslims questions about their faith? Yes, we can ask questions about their faith and other aspects of Islam. It is often wise to avoid debating theology as it is easy to get tied up in knots; for example it can be very difficult explaining to a Muslim about the Trinity. What can speak to people's hearts is sharing a personal testimony or answers to prayer. Give them the New Testament (not a complete Bible as they will start reading at Genesis) and pray that the Lord will reveal himself to them.

The Hidden Face Of Islam

There are many faces of Islam. There is traditional Islam which deals with questions of life, death, hell, eternity, believers and non believers. This is the Islam that we all know of. Alongside this goes a popular Islam, or the outworking of Islam on the ground, which is often known as "folk Islam". It could also be described as the day-to-day Islam of ordinary people.

Popular Islam is strange for a westerner to comprehend, as it is deals with a world full of spiritual beings or powers. It involves pirs (holy men), amulets, curses, demons, angels and spiritual forces as very much part of everyday life. Historically and up to this present day Friday prayers in some mosques include cursing prayers against Christians and Jews. If a Muslim wife does not want her husband to take a second wife she will often go to a pir and get him to initiate a curse to prevent it. In East London there are advertisements in newspapers and fliers dropped through letterboxes that offer to deal with everyday problems by putting a curse on a person, for a sum of money.

This is a different world, a world in which powers of evil are a reality. One such power is the evil eye, a force that Muslims believe can devastate lives. The fundamental concept of the evil eye is that anything that is precious, whether it be a person or a thing, is constantly vulnerable to hurt or destruction caused by other people's envy. Such envy or jealousy is projected by looking at the person or thing hence it is called the evil eye. These are forces that affect people's lives adversely.

At one of our meetings Joan sought me out to tell me the remarkable story of her friend Barbara. Her friend was a deeply committed Christian and had been one of the leaders in the Christian Union when she was at university. After university she met a Muslim man who had been in her class at school. After a short courtship, they got married. Barbara had only been married for eight months when she woke up suddenly one morning, startled awake by the horror-stricken thought: "What have I done?" She said that it was though something fell from her and in that moment she returned to her real self, the person she had been before her marriage. She believes that there was some demonic force or occult hold or curse that was affecting her life. It had suddenly broken and her mind was now clear and a weight had fallen off her. That day she packed her bags, left her Muslim husband and was divorced.

One of the first things that Muhammad did was to destroy crosses. In some Muslim countries today crosses are not allowed on churches and we often hear how the cross causes offence to Islam. Muslims believe in the second coming of Jesus, but they believe he will come as a Muslim and one of the first things he will do will be to destroy all crosses. Islam denies truths that are pivotal to the Christian faith including the death of Jesus on the cross, his resurrection, his deity, and that he is the Son of God, which they consider blasphemous.

How Do We Pray?

With regard to prayer, we have to realise that we are in a spiritual battle and need to pray accordingly. In the book of Ephesians 6:12 we read "For our struggle is not against flesh and blood, but against the rulers, against the authorities, against the powers of this dark world and against the spiritual forces of evil in the heavenly realms".

We have to love and care for Muslims and share the Gospel with them. But we need to be aware of the implications for us of having close contact with the religion of Islam. People become bound to Islam when they enter it and then are unable to see Christ. Their eyes become blindfolded to spiritual issues. Islam is an organised religion but there are also spiritual forces at work behind it, and these forces are not neutral forces but actively seek to oppose and destroy Christianity. We see this in the persecution of the Church in the Muslim world. For a Christian to go against these forces is really an encounter between Christ and Satan.

It is by prayer, intercession and releasing the forces that bind that we are able to see breakthroughs in the lives of those we love who are considering converting to Islam. Because of the finished work of Christ we have been given power and authority over the powers of darkness. We need to pray in the name of Jesus and with the blood of Jesus that the forces of evil will be lifted and that the person will be released. In Zechariah 4:6 it says "'Not by might, nor by power but by my Spirit' says the Lord".

Conclusion

Over the years I have known many women who have married Muslims and have heard of many more. In the majority of cases the marriage does not continue or end well. The heart is such a deceiver: at the start of a relationship we can look at things on the surface and they seem so attractive and alluring, but the reality can be a pathway of destruction and sorrow. It is very painful to have to extricate oneself from such an experience and deal with the feelings of failure and worthlessness. But sometimes women have found that it is better to get out and to start afresh.

The consequences of letting passion override rational judgement have been a common theme in literature. Women should beware of taking any major life decisions when they are in this giddy state of love and sexual attraction. When women marry Muslims they can be so in the throes of romantic love that they get carried away and don't think objectively of the implications of differences in culture and religion on the marriage and the impact of this on the children.

Western women can be deceived into marrying Muslim men for purposes that are not innocent, and not for her best interests. They can be deliberately targeted for marriage, and even though someone is absolutely sure that this is not the case in their circumstances, many women have thought this and been wrong. There can also be some deception over the man's past. Muslim men are usually married before the age of thirty, so an apparently single man who is older than this could already have a wife or a secret past. The very fact that a man wants to marry soon after meeting or have a secret wedding could mean that he has something to hide or an ulterior motive for the marriage.

The cultural gulf is very wide between western and Islamic culture. Many women simply don't realise that Muslim men will have deeply embedded cultural norms and expectations in their psyche that they will find virtually impossible to change. Many women think that their men will change with marriage or that they can change them, but this is seldom the case. It is far more likely to be the woman who will have to adapt and take the man's culture.

A woman who marries a Muslim will not be able to behave in the same way as her western counterparts, as her whole life will be subjected to the "honour and shame" principle. She will not have the freedom in her friendships to discuss openly any of her difficulties or problems, as that would bring shame on the family. She will be unable to have conversation or any form of friendship with a member of the opposite sex, as this will be perceived as "having an affair". She will have to accept that with her children, the boys will be considered more important and have a higher status in Muslim society. She will have to realise that it is her husband who has the authority within the family and she will face restrictions on any attempt of self expression.Many Muslim men are marrying western women considerably older than themselves, with an age difference of fifteen or more years being not unusual. However it is considered inappropriate in Islamic culture for a wife to be older than her husband, and this is frowned upon. A woman considering marrying a younger Muslim man should ask herself, "Why is he marrying me?"

Many women do not realise that when they marry a Muslim it is the usual custom for the couple to go and live with his parents in their home. Here she will have to do all the household chores and cooking under the watchful eye of the mother-in-law, and in many homes is considered no more than a slave. What is never mentioned is that in some Muslim cultures, a husband has greater love for his mother than his wife, and that is where his allegiance and loyalty lie.

Converting to Islam has repercussions on family and friends. Families can perceive it as dividing them or putting a wedge between family members. A mother may find it very difficult to accept a daughter who has become a Muslim and starts to wear all-concealing Islamic dress, such as the *burqa*. She may feel as if she has lost her daughter.

It is increasingly common when a girl marries a Muslim

man for her to start cutting herself off from her family. It often begins gradually and can signal deterioration in the marriage or the husband becoming more conservative and demanding. The husband might insist that she wears a *hijab* or *burqa* or he might confine her increasingly to the home. He might demand that she breaks off contact with her family. All this can be very distressing both for herself and her family who do not understand what is going on. The wife can be very fearful of what is happening within her marriage and too frightened to tell anybody. One woman I have heard of, who is experiencing these kinds of distressing pressures, has found it very difficult to eat and is losing weight. If this situation occurs it would be prudent to visit the person during the day when the husband is at work, but it is essential that contact and dialogue is maintained.

The Christian Teaching

These days many Christians tend to forget or discard the traditional teaching that a Christian should not marry a non-Christian. We read in the Bible in 2 Corinthians 6 verse 14:

Do not be yoked together with unbelievers.

And in Amos 3 verse 3:

Do two walk together unless they have agreed to do so?

Marrying someone who is not a Christian means that there are whole areas in life that cannot be shared, and they are vitally important areas. Also it does not bring the blessing of God. While acknowledging the dilemmas of single Christian women who long for marriage and children but find they greatly outnumber single men in the Church, marrying a

Muslim is never the answer.

If we are concerned about the number of Christians converting to Islam and want to stop this happening, it is necessary for pastors, parents and church leaders to make sure every Christian is educated about their own faith and the beliefs of others. It is only by people understanding both Christianity and Islam and the differences between them that this tide can be stemmed. Churches need to be making sure every member has thorough Bible teaching, so people are able to understand the tenets of their faith. We need to return to clear teaching of Christian theology in our churches, to enable people to be strong enough in their faith to withstand the encounters with different faiths and worldviews they are sure to have in today's world.

Comparing The Differences Between Islam And Christianity

As Islam increasingly confronts us in our modern world it becomes necessary to understand the differences between Islam and Christianity. This concise table of the main traditional beliefs in each religion is designed to make our understanding easy. For many people both religions appear similar, but are they really? Do they share the same prophets? Does each teach the same about Jesus? This helpful table addresses these and other important differences.

ISLAM

CHRISTIANITY

THE QUR'AN

It has 114 chapters (suras) and is roughly the size of the New Testament. The suras are put together in order of length, the longest ones at the beginning and the shortest at the end, except the first one The Opening (*al-Fatihah*). Muslims believe this book is uncreated, eternally preserved on a tablet in heaven, known as the 'Mother of the Book' (Sura 85:21-22). It was communicated word-for-word to Muhammad in Arabic over a period of 23 years (Sura 12:1-2). Muslims believe the angel Gabriel, sent by Allah, visited Muhammad with the revelations (Sura 26:193).

It is considered by Muslims to be the ultimate error-free authority on Islam.

The Qur'an is considered the final revelation of Allah to mankind, after the Torah (*Taurat*) of Moses, the Psalms (*Zabur*) of David and the Gospel (*Injil*) of Jesus. Muslims say that these scriptures (except the

THE BIBLE

It consists of 66 books written over a period of 1500 years by over 40 authors in Hebrew, Aramaic and Greek.

They wrote under the inspiration of the Holy Spirit: *'...no prophecy of Scripture came about by the prophet's own interpretation. For prophecy never had its origin in the human will, but prophets, though human, spoke from God as they were carried along by the Holy Spirit'* (2 Peter 1:20-21).

The Bible is the infallible word of God and is the ultimate authority for Christians.

ISLAM	CHRISTIANITY

The Qur'an (Cont.)

Qur'an) have been corrupted over time by the Jews and Christians.

Muslims believe that the Bible and all other scriptures have been superseded by the Qur'an.

Many of the revelations in the Qur'an are contradictory. Some of these are overcome by the Doctrine of Abrogation. This means that many of the suras that were revealed earlier in Muhammad's life are superseded by those that were revealed at a later date (Suras 2:106, 13:39).

ALLAH (GOD)

God is known as Allah. He is absolute oneness (*tawheed*). Sura 112 states 'He is Allah, the One and Only.

To put anyone or anything equal to Allah is the sin of *shirk* (polytheism). Therefore he has no equal partner, children or son and therefore there is no Trinity (*tathlith*) (Sura 4:171).

Muslims are in confusion with the Christian Trinity as they believe it is God the father, Mary the mother and Jesus the son (Sura 5:116).

GOD

God is one in an eternal Trinity, made up of the Father, Son and Holy Spirit. Not three gods, rather a unity of the Godhead: *'In the beginning God...', 'Therefore go and make disciples of all nations, baptising them in the name of the Father and of the Son and of the Holy Spirit'* (Gen 1:1, Matt 28:19).

ISLAM	CHRISTIANITY
ALLAH IS NOT A GOD OF LOVE Allah is not a god of love. He does not love sinners (Suras 2:276, 3:57, 4:107).	**GOD IS LOVE** God is love. Christ died for sinners because God loves mankind: *'For God so loved the world that He gave His one and only Son, that whoever believes in Him shall not perish but have eternal life'. 'But God demonstrates his own love for us in this: While we were still sinners Christ died for us'* (John 3:16, Rom 5:8).
ALLAH IS NOT FATHER Allah is unknowable and is not referred to as 'father'. He is transcendent (*tanzih*) and powerful.	**GOD IS FATHER** God has adopted those who believe on His Son as his heavenly children: *'Dear friends, now we are children of God'* (1 John 3:2). God is a knowable, heavenly father. He is transcendent and imminent; full of grace and glory: *'"Am I only a God nearby" declares the Lord, "and not a God far away? Who can hide in secret places so that I cannot see them?" declares the Lord. "Do not I fill heaven and earth?" declares the Lord'* (Jeremiah 23:23-24).

ISLAM	CHRISTIANITY
ALLAH IS CREATOR Allah is the creator of the world (Suras 23:14, 6:102, 13:16).	**GOD IS CREATOR** God is almighty, the Creator and sustainer of the world (Gen 1:1, 148:5).

ALLAH HAS NOT REVEALED HIMSELF TO MANKIND
    Allah is self-sufficient (Sura 31:26).
    Allah predetermines everything; the destiny of creation is fixed (Suras 25:2, 65:3). He determines all according to his mercy and wisdom (Suras 2:216, 42:27). All things are decreed by Allah (Sura 85:16). He can decree both good and evil.
	GOD HAS REVEALED HIMSELF IN JESUS
	He has revealed Himself to mankind in the person of Jesus: 'Jesus answered: *"...Anyone who has seen me has seen the Father"'* (John 14:9).

ATTRIBUTES AND ACTIONS Allah is best understood from his traditional 99 most beautiful names (Sura 7:180) although there are more than 99 found in the Qur'an. For example, they reveal his attributes: holy, eternal, the one, the hidden, the manifest, the light, the most high, the omniscient, the living, the omnipotent, the seeing, the hearing, the wise, the dominator, the strong and the crafty one (Suras 3:54, 8:30). And they reveal his actions:	**ATTRIBUTES AND ACTIONS** God is described in the Bible as eternal, glorious, almighty, merciful, holy, righteous, forgiving, omnipotent, incomparable and omniscient. And his actions are loving, just and wise.

ISLAM	CHRISTIANITY
Attributes And Actions (cont.) the guide, the provider, the gentle, the just, the merciful, the harmer, the withholder, the avenger, the abaser and the one who leads astray (Sura 6:39). **Some of Allah's actions and attributes are not consistent with the Biblical God.**	

JESUS (Isa)

In the Qur'an, Jesus' name is 'Isa', and is often called 'Isa son of Mary'. In most places he is called 'apostle of Allah'(Sura 3:49), but also 'servant of Allah' (Sura 19:30), the 'Masih'(the 'Messiah', but not in the specific Biblical meaning) (Sura 3:45), 'a sign for mankind'(Sura 19:21), a 'word of Allah' (Sura 4:171) and 'a spirit from him'(Sura 21:91).

JESUS

The Bible has many names for Jesus, some are: Creator, Saviour, the Word, Holy One, Image of God, Lord, Prince of Peace and Mediator.

VIRGIN BIRTH

Isa/Jesus was born of the virgin Mary, and was fully human (Sura 3:42-47).

VIRGIN BIRTH

Jesus was born of the virgin Mary and was fully human: *'the Word became flesh and made His dwelling among us'* (John 1:14).

ISLAM	CHRISTIANITY
JESUS IS NOT THE SON OF GOD Jesus is a created being and is only a man (Suras 3:59, 5:75). Jesus is not the son of God or divine (Suras 9:30, 19:34-35).	**JESUS IS THE SON OF GOD** Jesus is fully human and fully divine. He is the Son of God: *'And a voice from heaven said, "This is my Son, whom I love; with Him I am well pleased."'* (Matt 3:17, John 1:14, 18).
JESUS IS A PROPHET Jesus is a great prophet sent by Allah who is held in honour in this world and in the hereafter (Sura 3:45). He announces Muhammad as the next and last prophet (Sura 61:6)	**JESUS IS THE FULFILMENT OF THE PROPHETS** Jesus is the fulfilment of the law and the prophets: *'Do not think that I [Jesus] have come to abolish the Law of the Prophets; I have not come to abolish them but to fulfil them'* (Matt 5:17).
JESUS PERFORMED MIRACLES Jesus was a miracle-worker. 'With the permission of God' he made a clay bird come to life (the Arabic word *khalaqa* is used only for God's creating work). He healed, raised the dead and knew the unknown (Sura 3:49).	**JESUS PERFORMED MIRACLES** Jesus performed miracles during His earthly ministry to reveal His glory: *'This, the first of His miraculous signs, Jesus performed at Cana in Galilee. He thus revealed His glory, and His disciples put their faith in Him.'* (John 2:11). This included bringing the dead to life: *'...Jesus called in a loud voice, "Lazarus come out!" The dead man came out, his hands and feet wrapped with strips*

ISLAM	CHRISTIANITY
	Jesus Performed Miracles (cont.) *of linen, and a cloth around his face'* (John 11: 43-44).
JESUS DID NOT DIE ON THE CROSS OR RISE FROM THE DEAD Jesus did not die on a cross and he did not rise from the dead. Another man died in the place of Jesus on the cross. Muslims believe that Allah would not allow one of his prophets to die a death of disgrace (Sura 4:157).	**JESUS DIED ON THE CROSS AND ROSE AGAIN** Jesus died on a cross because of the sin of mankind. *'It was the third hour when they crucified Him'.* (Mark 15:25). He defeated death and was raised from the dead on the third day: *'When Jesus rose early on the first day of the week, he appeared to Mary Magdalene…'* (1 Cor 15:3-8, Rom 4:25).
JESUS ASCENDED INTO HEAVEN Muslims believe that Jesus ascended to heaven, where he still lives and will one day return (Suras 3:55, 4:157-8).	**JESUS ASCENDED INTO HEAVEN** He ascended into heaven and now sits at the right hand of God the Father until the second-coming: *'After the Lord Jesus had spoken to them, He was taken up into heaven and He sat at the right hand of God'* (Mark 16:19).

ISLAM	CHRISTIANITY
JESUS WILL COME AGAIN BUT AS A MUSLIM Jesus will return to earth as a Muslim at the second-coming, he will get married, have children, convert all Christians to Islam, some traditions say destroy the Jews, break all crosses, rule as king of the Muslims, kill all swine, die and be buried alongside Muhammad in Medina (*Sahih Muslim* vol 1, bk 1, c 71, p.104).	**JESUS WILL COME AGAIN AS KING OF KINGS AND LORD OF LORDS** *'They will see the Son of Man coming on the clouds of the sky, with power and great glory. And he will send his angels with a loud trumpet call, and they will gather his elect from the four winds, from one end of the heavens to the other'* (Matt 24:30-31).
HOLY SPIRIT The Quran speaks only very vaguely about a spirit, sometimes called 'holy spirit' (*rul al-qudus*) (Sura 16:102). Muslims identify him with angel Gabriel.	**HOLY SPIRIT** The Holy Spirit is part of the triune Godhead: *'Again Jesus said, "Peace be upon you! As the Father has sent me, I am sending you." And with that he breathed on them and said, "Receive the Holy Spirit"'* (John 20:21-22).
CREATION Allah created the heavens and the earth in six days (Suras 29:44, 50:38).	**CREATION** God created the universe in six days. *'In the beginning God created the heavens and the earth'* (Genesis 1:1).

ISLAM	CHRISTIANITY
CREATION OF MANKIND Allah created man from either clay or a blood-clot to worship and obey him (Suras 32:7, 96:2, 51:56). He asked his angels advice in the creation of man (Sura 2:30).	**CREATION OF MANKIND** God created man in his own image: *'So God created human beings in his own image, in the image of God he created them; male and female he created them'* (Genesis 1:27).
ADAM AND EVE CREATED WEAK Adam was created 'weak', i.e. not perfect (Sura 4:28).	**ADAM AND EVE CREATED SINLESS** God created Adam and Eve innocent and sinless.
THE FALL OF MAN The story of mankind's fall was actually an equal challenge between Allah and Satan (Suras 7:11-17, 24).Satan was disobedient to God because he did not prostrate before Adam. Adam and Eve got caught up in this challenge and were tempted by Satan in Paradise (Heaven).	**THE FALL OF MAN** Satan tempted Eve to sin. Eve then tempted Adam. They both disobeyed God and ate of the forbidden fruit: *'When the women saw that the fruit of the tree was good for food...she took some and ate it. She also gave some to her husband, who was with her, and he ate it'* (Gen 3:6). In Christianity Adam and Eve were tempted on earth.
THE RESULT OF THE FALL Adam and Eve repented and God accepted (Suras 2:37, 7:23). Adam and Eve were then cast down to earth without sin (Sura 2:36). Because	**THE RESULT OF THE FALL** This sin against God resulted in their expulsion from the earthly Garden of Eden and separation from God: *'So the Lord God banished him*

ISLAM	CHRISTIANITY
The Result Of The Fall (cont.)	**The Result Of The Fall (cont.)**
their sin was a personal lapse it did not bring innate sin on the whole of mankind.	[Adam] *from the Garden of Eden...'* (Gen 3:23). Their actions had the consequence of bringing sin into the world, which brought death. Man is a sinner and completely lost (Romans 6:23).
Therefore there is no need for a Saviour to pay the ransom for sin.	**Therefore to save mankind, there needed to be a second Adam (Jesus) who would be a blood-sacrifice, breaking the power of sin and healing the divide between God and mankind.**

AFTER DEATH

ISLAM	CHRISTIANITY
At death the angel Izra'il separates the soul from the body (Sura 32:11). In the grave there is an examination by the angels Munkar and Nakir, which sometimes involves torture. Prayer for the dead is beneficial (Sura 59:10). Between death and the Judgement Day (*yaum al-hisab*) the soul rests in purgatory (*barzakh*).	Christ will come again to judge the world. Only God the Father knows this appointed time. Christ will come as the King-of-Kings in power and splendour, heralded in by angels. The dead will be resurrected: *'At that time people will see the Son of Man coming in clouds with great power and glory. And He will send His angels and gather His elect from the four winds, from the ends of the earth to the ends of the heavens'* (Mark 13:26-27).

ISLAM   CHRISTIANITY

JUDGEMENT DAY (yaum ad-din)

The angel Israf'il will blow the trumpet (*sur*) to announce the last day. The dead will be resurrected (Sura 39:67-75). The balance of the good and bad deeds will be weighed. (Suras 21:47, 23:102-3). There will be a sharp bridge for all humanity to cross (the bridge of *sirat*) over hell fire. Those whose good deeds exceed the bad deeds will pass over it.

Salvation in Islam is through works, but there is no assurance and nothing can be guaranteed.

JUDGEMENT DAY

All must appear before the judgement seat of Christ. Those who did not put their faith in Christ will be judged with eternal punishment. For the Christian, it is only their works that will be judged: *'For we must all appear before the judgement seat of Christ, that everyone may receive what is due them for the things done while in the body, whether good or bad'* (2 Cor 5:10, John 3:18, Mt 25:31-46).

SIGNS OF THE END TIMES

Only Allah and Jesus know when the Judgement Day will be. Jesus has knowledge of the hour (Sura 43:61).

The signs of the last days are the lesser signs which are: an increase of injustice, sin, faithlessness, shamelessness and tribulation. The greater signs will be the Antichrist (*Dajjal*), the Beast of the earth, the rising of the sun in the West, the

SIGNS OF THE END TIMES

The signs of the end times include: wars, natural disasters, false prophets and an increase of sin in the world: *'"...many will come in my [Jesus] name, claiming 'I am the Christ', and will deceive many. You will hear of wars and rumours of wars, but see to it that you are not alarmed. Such things must happen, but the end is still to come. Nation will rise against nation...There will*

ISLAM	CHRISTIANITY
Signs Of The End Times (cont.) return of Jesus, Gog and Magog and also the appearance of the Mahdi. On Judgement Day all creatures will die and the universe will be destroyed. **There are many signs of the end times that are similar in both religions.**	**Signs Of The End Times (cont.)** *be famines and earthquakes...'''* (Matt 24:4-8). The earth will be burnt up with fire. There will be a new heaven and a new earth for the believers to dwell in: *'...for the first heaven and the first earth had passed away...'* (Rev 21:1).

| **SIN** Sin is disobedience to divine law. It is only accountable if done intentionally. There are major and minor sins. | **SIN** Sin is any failure to conform to the moral law of God in act, attitude or nature. |

| **HUMANS ARE NOT SINFUL** God found Muhammad astray (pre-inspiration Sura 93:7), Muhammad asked for forgiveness (Sura 47:19), God guided him and granted him forgiveness (Sura 48:2). Man is not innately sinful. Children are born sinless. Humans choose whether to sin or not. | **HUMANS ARE SINFUL BY THEIR NATURE** Man is innately sinful because he inherited the nature that came from the fallen first man (Adam). *'Therefore, just as sin entered the world through one man, and death through sin, and in this way death came to all people, because all sinned...'* (Rom 5:12). |

ISLAM	CHRISTIANITY
JESUS WAS FAULTLESS	**JESUS WAS SINLESS**
He said: 'I am only a messenger of thy Lord, that I may bestow on thee a faultless son' *(Sura 19:19)*.	Jesus was without sin, but God made him share our nature and on the cross became sin that we might share the righteousness of God: *'God made Him who had no sin to be sin for us, so that in Him we might become the righteousness of God'* (2 Cor 5:21).
SALVATION THROUGH WORKS	**SALVATION THROUGH FAITH**
Mankind must submit to Allah to find forgiveness. There is no atonement in Islam (Sura 17:15). There is no certainty in salvation because Allah 'forgives whom he pleases, and punishes whom he pleases' (Sura 2:284).	Salvation is by faith in the saving action of Jesus on the cross and not by works. God's grace is a free gift; people do not have to work to gain this gift of salvation: *'For it is by grace you have been saved, through faith – and this not from yourselves, it is the gift of God – not by works, so that no-one can boast'* (Eph 2:8-9). Good works are the fruit of this salvation.
Only works are taken into account. The Hadiths serve as a blue-print of how a Muslim should live his life. The Qur'an and Hadith give five obligatory duties for Muslims to perform. These five pillars are: the confession of faith, prayer, fasting, almsgiving and pilgrimage to Mecca.	By believing that Jesus died and rose again brings reconciliation with God, forgiveness of one's sins and assurance of salvation: *'…Their* [human] *sins and lawless acts I* [God] *will remember no more'* (Heb 10:17).
The way to salvation for a Muslim is by guidance (*huda*) and good works. There is no certainty.	

ISLAM	CHRISTIANITY
	Salvation Through Faith (cont.) In Christianity we have the certainty of salvation through Christ's atonement, not by good works.

HEAVEN (Paradise)

Paradise (*janna, firdous*) is a sensuous place of pleasure and joy. Allah will not be in fellowship with the righteous in paradise. The righteous will find there beautiful women (*houris*), full goblets of drink, rich carpets and couches (Suras 55:47-78, 56:11-38, 88:8-16). There will be a plentiful supply of food, fountains of drink and rivers of milk, wine and honey (Suras 47:15, 56:8-38). **In Islam heaven is a place of sensual delights and is not centred on Allah.**

Martyrs will have their sins blotted out by Allah and will enter into paradise immediately (Sura 3:169). There is no guarantee of direct entry into paradise for any other Muslim.

Women can only get to heaven by being completely obedient to their husbands. *Sahih Al Bukhari, 161:2*

HEAVEN

Heaven is a perfect place of eternal joy, worship and holiness, where God will be worshipped and served forever: *'the twenty-four elders fall down before Him who sits on the throne, and worship Him who lives for ever and ever...'* (Rev 4:10-11, 5:13).

In heaven there will be no pain, death or marriage: *'When the dead rise, they will neither marry nor be given in marriage'* (Mark 12:25).

Only those who have put their faith in Christ can enter heaven. They will be rewarded by God for their faithfulness.

ISLAM	CHRISTIANITY
HELL	**HELL**
Hell (*al-Nar or Jahannum*) is a place of fiery torment for sinners (Sura 78:21-30). Those in hell will 'neither die nor live' (Sura 87:13). There will be boiling water to drink and bitter food to eat (Sura 88:5-7).	The Bible presents hell as a place of eternal suffering and punishment: '*Then they* [those who do not know Christ] *will go away to eternal punishment, but the righteous to eternal life'*, *'...it is better for you to enter the kingdom of God with one eye than to have two eyes and be thrown in to hell, where...the fire is not quenched'* (Matt 25:46, Mark 9:47-48).
Hell will have 7 chambers. The first is purgatorial fire (*Jahannum*) for Muslims. The second is flaming fire (*Laza*) for Christians, which is not eternal. The third is the raging fire (*Hutama*) for Jews, which is not eternal (Sura 104:4). The fourth is the blazing fire (*Sa'ir*) for Sabians, which is not eternal (Sura 2:62). The fifth is the scorching fire (*Sakar*) for Zoroastrians. The sixth is the fierce fire (*Jahim*), for idolaters and polytheists which is eternal. The seventh is the abyss (*Hawiya*) for hypocrites (Sura 101:9).	Those who do not repent of their sin and believe in Christ will end up in hell: *'Jesus said to her* [Martha], *"I am the resurrection and the life. Those who believe in me will live, even though they die; and whoever lives and believes in me will never die. Do you believe this?"'* (John 11:25).
Muhammad intercedes for Muslims in purgatory (Sura 5:69).	**Through faith in Christ all Christians (men and women equally) have the certainty of heaven.**
In the Hadith it is recorded that Muhammad reported that hell would be full of poor people and women (Sahih Al Bukhari 301:1).	

ISLAM

CHRISTIANITY

PROPHETS

These are the people whom Allah chose and prepared to remind mankind of himself and to make known his commands. They are truthful, miracle-workers, sinless and infallible. Each had the same message and they were often treated badly by unbelievers (Sura 21: 25, 36).

Adam was the first prophet. Some more prominent prophets are: Noah, the preacher of Allah; Abraham, the friend of Allah; Moses, the speaker with Allah; John the Baptist and Isa (Jesus). There are three pre-Islamic prophets Hud, prophet to the ancient tribe of Ad, Salih, prophet to the tribe of Thamud and Shu'aib prophet to the tribe of Madyan. Muslims believe that Muhammad is the last and seal of the prophets. He is the greatest of the prophets (Suras 33:40, 61:6).

PROPHETS

The prophets of the Old and New Testament are chosen by God, not because of their sinless life but because of their obedience to God.

With all the prophets of the Old and New Testament Jesus is considered greater. *'In the past God spoke to our ancestors through the prophets at many times and in various ways, but in these last days He has spoken to us by His Son, whom He appointed heir of all things, and through whom He made the universe'* (Heb 1:1-2).

Jesus had apostles to help Him during His earthly ministry. They then took His Gospel to the world.

THE SONS OF IBRAHIM ISHMAEL & ISAAC

Hagar (*Hajar*), Abraham's (*Ibrahim's*) maid, gave birth to Ishmael. Sarah, his wife, gave birth to Isaac (Sura 14:39).

THE SONS OF ABRAHAM ISHMAEL & ISAAC

Hagar Abraham's maid gave birth to Ishmael and Sarah his wife gave birth to Isaac.

ISLAM	CHRISTIANITY
The Sons Of Ibrahim	**The Sons Of Ibrahim**
Ishmael & Isaac (cont.)	**Ishmael & Isaac (cont.)**
Tradition makes Ishmael the father of the Arab people as it was through his blood-line that Muhammad would be born.	*'Hagar* [Abraham's maid] *bore Abram a son, and Abram* [later named Abraham] *gave the name Ishmael to the son she had borne'* (Gen 16:15). *'Sarah* [Abraham's wife] *became pregnant and bore a son to Abraham in his old age, at the very time God had promised him. Abraham gave the name Isaac to the son Sarah bore him'* (Gen 21:2-3).
Muslims believe that Abraham and Ishmael built the cube-shaped Ka'aba (house of Allah) in Mecca. (Sura 2:124-5).	

ISHMAEL:THE SON OF THE SACRIFICE

Through Isaac's blood-line many prophets would be born, including David and Jesus. Muslims believe that Isaac was the son of promise but not the one to be sacrificed (Suras 11:69-73, 37:112-113).

Abraham's faith was tested by the order to sacrifice his son. Allah sent an angel with a ram that was sacrificed in the son's place (Sura 37:100-111). The Qur'an does not mention the name of the son, tradition mentions both sons, and from the middle ages they say it was Ishmael.

ISAAC:THE SON OF PROMISE

Isaac was the chosen son, from whose blood-line the Messiah would be born: *'Then God said, "Yes, but your* [Abraham's] *wife Sarah will bear you a son, and you will call him Isaac. I will establish my covenant with him as an everlasting covenant for his descendants after him'* (Gen 17:19).

As a test of faith, *'God said* [to Abraham], *"take your son, your only son, Isaac, whom you love, and go to the region of Moriah. Sacrifice him there as a burnt offering on one of the mountains I will tell*

ISLAM	CHRISTIANITY

Ishmael:the Son Of The Sacrifice (cont.)

Ishmael is regarded as a prophet (Sura 2:136). Abraham left Hagar and Ishmael in Mecca and Allah provided water for them to drink at a place called Zamzam. This place is visited today by Muslims on pilgrimage to Mecca.

Isaac:the Son Of Promise (cont.)

you about"' (Gen 22:2). At the last minute, God sent an angel to stop Abraham killing Isaac, by presenting him with a ram. Abraham withstood the test of his faith.

In the Bible it says that Abraham prepared to sacrifice his son Isaac, the son of promise, not Ishmael.

ANGELS

Angels were created out of fire by Allah (Sura 7:12). Their role is to protect believers, to praise Allah and to guard the Qur'an (Sura 3:124-5). They are intercessors who pray for the prophets and believers (Sura 33:43, 56).

The number of angels is not known, however four angels stand out: Jibr'il (Gabriel), Israf'il who blows his trumpet on Judgement Day, Mika'il (Michael) who brings the rain and Izra'il, the angel of death.

There are two angels that daily record the good deeds and the bad deeds of all humans (Sura 82:10-12).

ANGELS

Angels were created by God: *"For by him all things were created: things in heaven and on earth, visible and invisible"*(Col 1:16). They are called ministering spirits and God has commanded them to help men. *'Are not all angels ministering spirits sent to serve those who inherit salvation'* (Heb.1:14). They protect and deliver and guide our ways. They surround the throne of God, praise and serve him (Isaiah 6:1-6).

Millions of angels are at God's command. Michael is the archangel, Gabriel is one of the most prominent angels, and is God's messenger of mercy and promise. He always bears good news. *'The angel answered,*

ISLAM	CHRISTIANITY
	ANGELS (cont.) *"I am Gabriel, I stand in the presence of God, and I have been sent to speak to you and to tell you this good news'* (Luke 1:19).
SATAN Satan was an angel, but was disobedient to God and did not bow down to Adam and as a result was thrown out of heaven (Sura 2:34).	**SATAN** Satan was once an archangel. Before the creation of the earth he led a heavenly rebellion against God, and was cast out of heaven forever (Isaiah 14:12-15). After Judgement Day he and his fallen angels or demons will spend eternity in hell: *'Then He* [Jesus] *will say to those on His left, "depart from me, you who are cursed, into the eternal fire prepared for the devil and his angel" 'And the devil who deceived them, was thrown into the lake of burning sulphur…'* (Matt 25:41, Rev 20:10).
JINNS Jinn are beings between angels and men that Allah created from smokeless fire and belong to the spirit world (Sura 55:15). They were created to worship Allah (Sura 51:56). The jinn can beget children,	

ISLAM	CHRISTIANITY

Jinns (cont.)

possess humans, have an abode (e.g. trees) and can change form into cows, sheep, etc. Although theoretically neutral most jinn are considered bad. Jinn can be believers or non-believers (Suras (6:130, 72:1-17).

Satans (shaitans) are truth-concealing jinn, and Iblis (the Devil) is one (Sura 15:50). He is a jinn who leads evil jinn. Iblis is destined to be thrown into hell fire on Judgement Day.

FAITH	**FAITH**
Faith is the confession with the tongue that "there is no god but Allah, and Muhammad is his messenger," the internal conviction and the performing of the duties and obligations of the religion.	Faith is confessing that Jesus Christ is Lord and acknowledging that He died on the cross and rose from the dead. It is through this there is forgiveness of sins and eternal life. Faith is a personal and living relationship with God.